The Essential...
Taylor Swift

Published in 2024 by Gemini Editions Ltd,
part of the Gemini Books Group

Based in Woodbridge and London

Marine House,
Tide Mill Way, Woodbridge,
Suffolk, IP12 1AP

A CIP catalogue for this book is available from the British Library

ISBN 9781917082006

Printed in Europe

The Essential...
Taylor Swift

CAROLINE YOUNG

Contents

OPPOSITE
Taylor Swift, 2023.

Introduction

A car is traveling along a country road in upstate New York, winding through sun-speckled woodland, where the leaves are blazing red and gold. The driver of the car, a man in his twenties dressed in flannels and with a beard, can't stop looking over at the girl in the passenger seat, whose hair is the color of the fall leaves. She smiles back at him, and as she squeezes his hand tightly, she feels the overwhelming besottedness of this new relationship.

This scene is from Taylor Swift's short film that accompanied the ten-minute extended version of the song "All Too Well" on its release in October 2021. The video so clearly conveyed the lyrics, particularly in the opening moments. As the girl follows him into his family's house and soaks up these new surroundings that offer a hopeful glimpse of the future, she unwinds the red scarf from around her neck, and hangs it on the banister. For every Taylor Swift fan, this moment was everything.

From her debut album in 2007, Taylor's lyrics have become a puzzle to solve; none more so than in "All Too Well," which, by the time of the release of the short film, was firmly part of her lore.

The original song, from the 2012 album *Red*, was never a single, but it was a clear fan favorite for its perfectly crafted lyrics that chimed with all those who had felt the excruciating pain of a break-up. The power was in the lines that conveyed so much in their succinctness, from the joy of kitchen dancing to the pain felt during break-up phone calls. By the time of the release of *Red*, her fourth album, it had become an enjoyably addictive game to guess what, and who, her songs were about. While she didn't name names, she left clues like cakecrumbs in the liner notes for each album, hinting at the famous men who had broken her heart. And for "All Too Well," the hidden message within the song lyrics in *Red*'s album sleeve referred to maple lattes.

In the fall of 2010, celebrity gossip magazines were splashed with candid photos of Taylor walking the streets of Brooklyn with actor Jake Gyllenhaal on Thanksgiving. She had one arm draped around his puffer-jacket-clad shoulders, the other holding a Starbucks cup, and with a striped scarf wrapped around her neck. They were both in joyful, loved-up mode, laughing at each other's jokes and seemingly unaware that they were in the sight of photographers. In other photos, taken on the same day, Taylor was walking and chatting with Jake's sister, Maggie Gyllenhaal.

All these clues—the festive latte, the scarf, the visit to his sister's house—clearly linked her relationship with Jake to the lyrics in "All Too Well." The folkloric scarf is used as a device to frame the journey of the relationship, from being left at his sister's house, as homely as the blissful peak of a romance, to being kept in a drawer as a memento of regret. Maggie was even quizzed in interviews as to whether she really did have it. But the scarf wasn't as literal as had been interpreted. Taylor later revealed that the red scarf was a metaphor for the loss of virginity and the breaking of first love.

As she recounted to *Rolling Stone* in 2020, she was in the studio with her band, nursing the pain of her recent break-up, when she crafted the lyrics. She was so mad and emotionally drained, feeling like "a broken human," that she scrawled out words on paper until she'd created a ten-minute song. Afterwards, she called up songwriter Liz Rose to help her edit it down to a standard length for the album. It was never released as a single, yet it took on a life of its own, credited as a piece of genius songwriting, with *Rolling Stone*, in 2021, naming it one of the 500 greatest songs of all time.

Like the aesthetics of her short film, Taylor Swift is often considered cozy and comforting. She's pumpkin spice lattes and autumn leaves, she adores cats, she wears her heart on her sleeve, and she writes about love. As a teen country music star, she forged an "adorkable" persona, the nerdy girl who is pining for the cute guy, and in an early bio, as featured on her website, she described her favorite thing as "writing about life, specifically the parts of life concerning love. Because, as far as I'm concerned, love is absolutely everything."

OPPOSITE TOP Kanye West crashes Taylor's acceptance speech at the 2009 MTV Video Music Awards, a moment that would have a lasting impact on her career.

OPPOSITE BOTTOM LEFT At the CMT (Country Music Television) Music Awards in 2006.

OPPOSITE BOTTOM RIGHT Taylor Swift in 2010, around the time of the release of her third album, *Speak Now*.

THE ESSENTIAL... TAYLOR SWIFT

This tendency to sing about heartbreak and idealized love in fizzy pop songs and country ballads led to her nickname as "the queen of the break-up song," which allowed her to be dismissed as frivolous and non-serious for appealing to teenage girls, and for the negativity that comes with the overtly feminine. Even as she was breaking records and winning awards, she was ridiculed for writing songs about her real-life relationships, never mind that's what The Rolling Stones and Bob Dylan were doing in the sixties. It's the classic double standard for a female artist, whose life, and love life, is scrutinized endlessly. Throughout her career she has railed against the sexism that has touched her from the earliest moments in her stardom, describing how she was so often "slut-shamed" for being "man hungry," while at the same time being called a prude for not wishing to strip off for sexy photoshoots.

What's undoubtedly evident, and what those with internalized misogyny have often failed to appreciate, is the sheer breadth of her talent. Taylor is a poet and wordsmith who can fire off a hit record in an instant, where she tunes into her own emotions to capture universal feelings. Her music wouldn't have been so immensely

ABOVE Looking every bit the model in a Union Jack themed outfit, while performing at the 2013 Victoria's Secret Fashion Show.

popular, and she wouldn't have won twelve Grammys and forty American Music Awards, if it wasn't the case.

Her songwriting has been compared with Joni Mitchell and Bob Dylan, her lyrics on a par with the poetry of William Wordsworth (who she referenced in the beautifully haunting "The Lakes"). Her songs resonate with all those who have felt like outsiders, like they don't fit into society's neat boxes, and even though she's singing about her own experiences, they are relatable to people of all ages. There's a Taylor song for every mood: funny, upbeat, catchy Taylor, with "Shake It Off" and "We Are Never Getting Back Together" (often the first release from an album); heartbreaking Taylor ("All Too Well," "I Almost Do," "White Horse"); the Taylor who makes you catch your throat when she sings of loss and life's cruelty ("Ronan," "Soon You'll Get Better," "Bigger than the Whole Sky"); infectious Taylor, with synthy pop that you can't stop playing ("I Knew You Were Trouble" and "Cruel Summer"); the carnal ("False God," "Dress"); and the vengeful Taylor, where she helps you express your own desire for revenge ("Picture to Burn," "Karma," "Mad Woman").

From, at the age of thirteen, being the youngest artist signed by the Sony/ATV publishing house to having sold 114 million albums as of 2023, she has been a consistent force of talent driven by ambition and hard work. As a young country star, she followed the tradition of country music in always embracing her audience, connecting with them on MySpace and on her website—an internet baby using the new tools to forge a community—and treating them as friends, rather than just fans, as they grew into a behemoth of "Swifties."

She was all too aware that in the fickle music business, she needed to keep changing, as young female musicians were considered replaceable (as reflected in "Nothing New"). She infused country with soft rock and dubstep elements into *Red*,

and then shifted into an eighties synth sound with *1989*, an album that dominated the pop charts and launched her as a pop cultural icon. There was her darker, revenge-laden *Reputation*, the softer, color-infused *Lover*, and then there were her lockdown cottagecore albums. During the global pandemic, she released *Evermore* and *Folklore*, and gained a whole new audience who enjoyed the folk sound and collaborations with musicians like Bon Iver.

"I've been raised up and down the flagpole of public opinion so many times in the last 20 years. I've been given a tiara, then had it taken away," she told *Time* in 2023. Yet she always chose to fight, even at times when she came up against powerful figures.

At the MTV Video Music Awards in 2009, as she was collecting her award for Best Female Video for "You Belong with Me," Kanye West stormed the stage, grabbed the microphone, and declared her an unworthy winner. She was a relative newcomer, just nineteen, and she looked stunned and upset at the intrusion. It was a moment that would have a lasting impact on her career, but she refused to be intimidated when she faced up against powerful figures like West, his then-wife Kim Kardashian, and record executive Scooter Braun.

PAGE 14-15

An homage to her albums, the Eras Tour is the first in music history to surpass $1 billion in revenue.

When her original record label, Big Machine, sold her first six records to Braun without her knowledge, she at first felt powerless not to have control of her own music. But then, in a ground-breaking, monumental move, she decided to re-record each one and release them with bonus songs "From the Vault" to give listeners a reward for playing Taylor's version rather than the original. The result? Some of the re-recorded versions were an even bigger success than the originals. It proved to be a way of regaining control of her music and to take revenge on those who "stripped me of my life's work."

Taylor is a billion-dollar businesswoman who has become the savior of the music industry, or, as Bloomberg boldly claimed in 2014, she is "The Music Industry." She's the top-played artist on Spotify and Apple Music, and the highest-grossing female performer of all time. She is her own CEO, one of the best marketing experts, with an awareness of her own brand and how to promote it via the internet.

On the release of *1989*, she was a trailblazer in trademarking the catchiest phrases from her lyrics to protect them from unauthorized merchandising.

> "I've been raised up and down the flagpole of public opinion so many times in the last 20 years. I've been given a tiara, then had it taken away."

When she released *Midnights*, her tenth studio album, in October 2022, she further rewarded fans by issuing collectible vinyl with different color themes, special editions with bonus tracks, and coveted merchandise. In just three days she shattered modern-day sales records and sold more than one million copies. After the release of *Speak Now (Taylor's Version)* in July 2023, she became the first female artist to have four albums in the *Billboard* 200 chart's Top Ten—with *Midnights*, *Lover*, and *Folklore*. She's also had more No. 1 albums in the *Billboard* 200 chart than any other woman, including Barbra Streisand.

Her astonishing success was evidenced with the sweeping grandeur of the Eras Tour, which kicked off in early 2023 and took in sixty dates in North America, before traveling to South America and Europe. After seeing the Eras Tour concert in Tampa, Florida, Billy Joel compared her to the "phenomenon of Beatlemania."

THE ESSENTIAL... TAYLOR SWIFT

It was estimated that after completing 151 stadium dates in 2024, ticket sales could exceed $1.4 billion.

Despite all this, she hasn't drifted away from her fans; she's the big sister who invites them to album launches in her homes and rewards them with her "Easter eggs." These clues began in the notes on her early albums, then expanded to Instagram posts and music videos, and in the microscopic analysis of her life, they help create a jigsaw of motifs and phrases that piece together significant moments.

Taylor's space is a community, a place with insider jokes and references, and where friendship bracelets are worn and exchanged, just as she did at her first gigs. There's a sense of belonging here, an understanding of the frailty of human feeling, and of the temporary in our connections. The emotional world that Taylor Swift has created is expressed in sheer color—the lavender haze, the maroon of lips and bruises, the golden memories, the ocean blue of a lover's eyes and the distance between them, and the blazing red of fall leaves, of love at its most passionate, and of a scarf left behind.

CHAPTER ONE
THE EARLY YEARS

" **H** i, I'm Taylor. I love the number 13. I was born in December on a Christmas tree farm. I like imagining what life was like hundreds of years ago." These were the words that Taylor once used to introduce herself on her website. In this one sentence, she conveyed so much about her persona: the friendly approachability, the favorite number that stemmed from her date of birth and a series of "weird coincidences," her early home life where it was Christmas every day, and a creative need for storytelling and expressing her emotions, which she would find in songwriting.

Taylor Alison Swift was born in West Reading, Pennsylvania, on December 13, 1989, to Andrea, who worked in marketing, and Scott, a stockbroker with Merrill Lynch. "It was such a weird place to grow up," she said in 2014 of the Christmas tree farm that they called their home. "But it has cemented in me this unnatural level of excitement about fall and then the holiday season. My friends are so sick of me talking about autumn coming. They're like, 'What are you, an elf?'"

She adored her early years on the farm, running around barefoot, and helping her parents out by doing chores with her younger brother, Austin. Because she was too little to lug the trees, she was tasked with picking the praying-mantis pods off the branches so they wouldn't hatch in people's homes. "It was just the most amazing, magical way to grow up," she would say of the place that fired up her imagination from an early age. She captured that enchantment in her Christmas anthem, "Christmas Tree Farm." The comfort of lying in her lover's arms, and of kissing under the mistletoe, transports her back to the sparkling winter wonderland

of the farm. She wrote in one of her profiles on MySpace that she loves things "that make me feel seven again," harking back to that special, magical time, also conveyed in the song "Seven."

She had a particularly tight bond with her mother, and in "The Best Day," one of the touching tracks from *Fearless*, she sings of her fond memories of being five years old, and of her doting parents and her younger brother, all of whom were supportive and loving.

In "I Bet You Think About Me," one of the "From the Vault" tracks from *Red (Taylor's Version)*, she describes her background as humble. Although they were financially comfortable from her father's investment work, it was a warm and grounded home life, where their tight bond meant her parents would always nurture her creativity, without being pushy. She had known, "ever since I was born," that all she wanted to do was sing. "There are videos of me walking up to strangers and singing songs from *The Lion King* when I was a baby," she told *The Philadelphia Inquirer* in 2007.

One of the major influences in her life was her maternal grandmother, Marjorie Finlay, a celebrated opera singer whose

ABOVE It's a family affair. From L-R: Austin Swift (brother), Taylor Swift, Andrea Finlay (mom), and Scott Swift (dad) walk together in New York City, 2014.

career offered an inspiring template, and who guided the young Taylor to express herself through music. Taylor dedicated the thirteenth track on *Evermore* to Marjorie (with thirteen being Taylor's age at the time of her grandmother's death), who she said, "still visits me sometimes . . . if only in my dreams." In the music video for "Wildest Dreams," Taylor based her character, an actress, on her grandmother—sporting the same sleek dark 1950s waves in her hair, and with the cinema marquee naming her as Marjorie Finn. She told radio DJ Zane Lowe, "My mom will look at me so many times and say 'God, you're just like her.'"

> "My dad, my mom, and my brother come up with some of the best ideas in my career. I always joke that we're a small family business."

There was a whole mix of music in the Swift household. Her mother listened to Def Leppard when she was pregnant with Taylor, and she would continue to blast out the English rock band throughout her childhood. While Taylor was similarly devoted to them, in "Begin

Again," she describes her obsession with James Taylor, who she was named after, and she was also drawn to female country musicians. LeAnn Rimes was an early love, and having been given her first album when she was six, she was an inspiration in having a music career at a young age.

In 1997, when Taylor was seven, the family moved from Pine Ridge Farm to Wyomissing, where they lived in an impressive "Georgian Colonial" villa at 78 Grandview Boulevard. She enrolled at the Wyomissing Area Junior High School, but it wouldn't be a happy time. She felt awkward and chubby as she was targeted and ostracized by bullies who decided "I was weird and they didn't like my hair."

"It was a really lonely time in my life," she added in an interview in 2007. "I was friends with a group of girls, and then I wasn't friends with them anymore, and I didn't know why. So you can translate that into really bad things in your life and let it drag you down, and do drugs or whatever, or you can find something good that lifts you above it. So I'm thankful that I found music at that time in my life."

ABOVE LEFT Taylor with her father, Scott, in 2008.

ABOVE RIGHT Taylor enjoys an incredibly close relationship with her mom, Andrea. Pictured here at the Country Music Awards, 2010.

THE ESSENTIAL... TAYLOR SWIFT

As well as her mass of blonde curls and her height, what made her stick out was her single-mindedness in her desire to be a singer. At the age of ten she was given a twelve-string guitar, and she practiced on it until her fingers bled. With her parents' support, she performed in Wyomissing karaoke contests and at county fairs, doing covers of The Dixie Chicks, Shania Twain, and Faith Hill. She was also given the chance to sing the national anthem at a Philadelphia 76ers baseball game in April 2002—a great way to get exposure in front of a sold-out crowd.

Once she'd mastered the guitar, she began putting down words to the music. She'd already been crafting poetry, winning a national contest when she was nine, so songwriting was a natural evolution. The first song she wrote, when she was twelve, was an upbeat anthem called "Lucky You," hinting at her ability to create upliftingly catchy hooks. The second original song, "The Outside," later featured on her debut album, was a more reflective track inspired by her own feelings of loneliness, of walking down the corridor at school not knowing who she could talk to that day. With this song, she said, "I was writing exactly what I saw. I was writing from pain."

Rather than getting drunk at parties like her peers, she preferred to attend singer-songwriter evenings—something which made her fundamentally uncool. Feeling like an outsider would be a constant theme in her music, as she wrote of escaping the small town that stifled her, and where she used the pain as a purpose. "The thing about being a songwriter is that no matter what happens, if you write a song about it, it's productive," she said.

The Swift family summers were spent at their second home in Stone Harbor, a wealthy Atlantic resort on the tip of New Jersey. Andrea would ask the owner of the local café, Coffee Talk, if Taylor could perform acoustic. The blonde-haired, chatty-but-serious girl would charm the customers as they sipped coffees, unaware they were hearing some of the earliest songs by a musical superstar. "My dad, my mom, and my brother come up with some of the best ideas in my career," she later reflected. "I always joke that we're a small family business." She was savvy enough at the age of twelve to snap up the taylorswift.com domain, with the foresight that she could use her website to market herself, further helping her gain traction.

Buoyed by some early success, she and her mother would go on road trips to Nashville, Tennessee, so she could hand out her demo tapes to record labels. Nashville was the home of country music. It was the place where her icons Faith Hill and LeAnn Rimes had found their sounds, and the music also allowed a creativity of expression, with raw and unflinching lyrics about love and loss. "I think all country music speaks to me," she said.

Having been shunned by her classmates, she didn't think being told no by adults would be any worse. So, the bold twelve-year-old knocked on Music Row office doors, saying, "Hi, I'm Taylor! I write songs and I think you should sign me."

The hard work paid off when, at thirteen, she became the youngest musician to be signed to the Sony/ATV Tree publishing house, as part of an RCA development deal to nurture young artists. To make it easier to cultivate her career, the family made the permanent move to Nashville, with her dad transferring to the local office of Merrill Lynch. She was featured in Abercrombie & Fitch's "Rising Stars" national campaign as one of twenty-seven up-and-coming young celebrities, where she was photographed with a guitar slung around her neck, while dabbing tears with a tissue. Further, "The Outside" was selected for a *Chicks with Attitude* compilation CD as a tie-in with a Maybelline beauty line and ad campaign.

Now enrolled at Hendersonville High School, much of her experience here influenced her early albums. On the first day of freshman year she sat next to a red-headed girl, Abigail, in English class, and the two would become best friends, encouraging each other's ambitions. She still felt like an ugly duckling, but now that she was in high school, she and Abigail accepted "we were never going to be popular, so we should just stick together and have fun and not take ourselves too seriously."

She was fifteen when she met Abigail, and fifteen when she had her first boyfriend, and these experiences formed the basis of one of her most powerful early songs, "Fifteen." It captured the loneliness and confusion of teen love and dreaming of dating the boy on the football team. Yet the character in this song, as in later hits "Mean" and "You're on Your Own, Kid," has a greater destiny ahead of her, outside of the small-town mindset.

OPPOSITE With early songwriting mentor Liz Rose at the 2010 Grammy Awards, where their co-write "White Horse" won best country song.

LEFT Arriving at the CMA's in 2007 wearing a sundress and cowboy boots. Along with her mass of curly hair, this becomes her first signature style.

RIGHT Taylor Swift, 2006.

She found it freeing to be in Nashville, where "all of the sudden I was a normal kid," although at the end of the school day, rather than after-school clubs, she would head over to RCA to work with established Music Row songwriters. Aware that her young age might hinder her in being taken seriously, she ensured she was always prepared for her meetings, arriving armed with a handful of solid ideas. One of these writers, Liz Rose, later said that these sessions were "some of the easiest I've ever done. Basically, I was just her editor. She'd write about what happened in school that day. She had such a clear vision of what she was trying to say. And she'd come in with the most incredible hooks."

Despite the achievement of her songwriting deal, she made the difficult decision to leave RCA when she realized she might not be allowed to perform her own songs. "I didn't want to just be another girl singer. I wanted there to be something that set me apart. And I knew that had to be my writing," she said. Writing meant everything to her, and given her clear focus, leaving this big record label was a risk she was willing to take.

CHAPTER TWO

THE FIRST ALBUMS

In Nashville, the rite of passage for every musician is the Bluebird Café, a place where songwriters are given the opportunity to play their own songs on the same stage as established country music stars. It was where country legends Garth Brooks, Keith Urban, and Faith Hill performed before they were famous, and on November 4, 2004, fourteen-year-old Taylor Swift took her seat on a stool on the stage. In front of a backdrop of photos of country stars, she performed a small set, including the as yet unreleased "Me and Britney" and "Beautiful Eyes."

Sitting in the audience was Scott Borchetta, a record executive who was in the process of launching his new label, Big Machine Records, and he was struck by the stage presence and songwriting talent of the teenager. He thought, "This girl has the potential to be a really big star. Her songs have these extraordinary takes on everyday life. There's a certain slant, a sense of humor and a sarcasm to them."

She became one of the label's first signings, and after sessions with producer Nathan Chapman and songwriter Liz Rose, she released her debut single, "Tim McGraw," on June 19, 2006. It was a nostalgic ballad about the power of music, and of a country song that holds a special place in a doomed relationship. Using the name of Tim McGraw, the country superstar and husband of Faith Hill, was a clever marketing tool to draw in listeners, and the song's sweet melody and lyrics earned positive reviews.

Her eponymous debut album, *Taylor Swift*, was released on October 24, 2006. She had co-writing credits on every track, with three as the sole writer, and the tracklist included "The Outside,"

one of her very first songs. It sold a modest 39,000 copies in its first week, but the momentum grew as she released further singles "Teardrops on My Guitar" and "Our Song" and gained more press coverage. The album topped the country album charts and peaked at No. 5 on the US *Billboard* 200, spending 157 weeks there—the longest for any album in the 2000s. It wasn't the only record she broke. She was the first female country music artist to co-write every track on a million-selling debut album. *The New York Times* described it as "a small masterpiece of pop-minded country."

With her glittery eyeshadow, lip-gloss smile, and sundresses worn with cowboy boots, she was marketed to a fresh demographic for country music—teenage girls. This was further buoyed by her intimate connection with her fans, both inperson and online. She always took the time for meet-and-greets, to sign autographs, and later, when cell phones were ubiquitous, to do selfies.

In the mid-2000s, country music hadn't realized the power of the internet, but Taylor was one of the first to take advantage of it, as she used MySpace and her website to speak to her audience directly. Most stars had a PR manager who would do the communications

THE ESSENTIAL... TAYLOR SWIFT

for them, but it was Taylor typing out her blogs, revealing her love
for baking experiments, cats, and television shows *CSI* and *Law &
Order*, and responding directly to her fans. This all helped to make
her record the best-selling country album of 2007. When she wrote
on her blog that she couldn't wait to meet them in person, "whether
it's in a crowd or a coffee shop," it felt completely sincere.

From these first songs, including the punchy "Picture to Burn,"
there were whispers among Hendersonville's teens as to who she was
singing about. The ode to revenge on an ex boyfriend who drove
pick-ups he never let her drive was said to be about a boy she dated
in her freshman year. Then there was her first serious boyfriend, who
inspired the longing in "Tim McGraw" as he was two years older and
due to go to college. "Our Song," a clever and upbeat ditty in which
the sounds of a small Southern town create the soundtrack to a loved-
up couple, was similarly based on her very real romantic feelings.

It wasn't just boys; "Tied Together with a Smile" was about one
of her friends, "a gorgeous, popular girl in high school. Every guy
wanted to be with her, every girl wanted to be her. I wrote that song
the day I found out she had an eating disorder."

She conceded, "I tend to be kind of blatantly obvious, and with my songs, I'll even mention names a lot of times." Although she also admitted, there were "definitely a few more people who think that I've written songs about them than there actually are."

By giving her listeners such access to her inner thoughts, and to her intimate relationships, it created a sense of authenticity. In the age of intense paparazzi and gossip sites, it was a clever marketing tool that came across as an uncalculated, organic decision.

Taylor was a sophomore when her debut album was released, and on the back of its huge success she switched from the classroom to being home-schooled on her tour bus. Her schedule was now packed with opportunities to perform at awards shows, as a support act for Rascal Flatts in late 2006 and for Brad Paisley over the summer of 2007.

> "This girl has the potential to be a really big star. Her songs have these extraordinary takes on everyday life. There's a certain slant, a sense of humor and a sarcasm to them."

Touring and performing was an adult world, but when she came home to Nashville, she returned to her life as a schoolgirl, where "my friends are 17. To them I'm just a 17-year-old. It's kind of interesting how you can lead a double life."

In her profile in *Time* magazine in 2023, she recounted a story of the early years starting out. She'd been booked to open for Kenny Chesney on his tour, a highly coveted spot that would be the highlight of her career. But a few weeks later she was told that because it was sponsored by a beer brand, she would be too young to be part of it. She was devastated. Later, on her eighteenth birthday, she received a card from Chesney, which included a check as a thoughtful gift to make up for her having to drop out of the tour. "It was for more money than I'd ever seen in my life," she said. "I was able to pay my band bonuses. I was able to pay for my tour buses. I was able to fuel my dreams."

In May 2007, she traveled to Las Vegas to perform at her first awards show, the forty-second Academy of Country Music Awards, where she performed "Tim McGraw" in front of the man himself. She followed it in November 2007 with a performance of "Our Song" at the Country Music Awards, where she won the Horizon

Award for best newcomer. She thanked her family for taking the chance to move to Nashville, country music radio for believing in her, and her fans for changing her life. "This is definitely the highlight of my senior year," she said.

Another highlight would be at the 2008 Grammy Awards, where she was nominated for Best New Artist but lost out to Amy Winehouse, who had a darker, grittier persona that was opposite of Taylor's earnestness. The American teen didn't balk at being a role model. She said that her point of reference in making decisions "is the 6-year-old girl in the front row of my concert. I think about what she would think if she saw me do what I was considering doing. Then I go back and I think about her mom and what her mom would think if I did that."

If her first album had made a big impact, her second, *Fearless*, would see her fame rise even further when it was released on November 11, 2008. The title referred to the embracing of new things, and of not being afraid to take a risk even if you're scared. It was promoted as a major record for the 2008 holiday season, and in anticipation, Ellen DeGeneres devoted a whole episode of her daytime talk show to an album launch party.

Taylor was a perfect interviewee on shows like *Ellen*, as she had a bubbly, friendly personality. She had the looks and style, with a clear talent and passion for music, and she wasn't ashamed to speak as a real, feeling, heartbroken teenager. In the first example of her being teased for her love life, Ellen displayed a picture of Taylor with Joe Jonas on the screen. "That's ouch," Taylor responded, and she tantalizingly revealed he'd broken up with her in a twenty-seven-second phone call.

Swift's summer 2008 romance with Joe Jonas, of pop group the Jonas Brothers, was the inspiration for the track "Forever and Always," which was written toward the very end of *Fearless*'s recording process. She begged Borchetta to allow her to add it to the final version of the album, as it conveyed all her confusion and heartbreak over him ending the relationship unexpectedly: "That emotion of rejection, for me, usually starts out sad and then gets mad. This song starts with this pretty melody that's easy to sing along with, then in the end . . . I'm basically screaming it because I'm so mad. I'm really proud of that."

While *Taylor Swift* had led to rumors in Hendersonville as to who her songs were about, this time they would be linked to

THE ESSENTIAL... TAYLOR SWIFT

OPPOSITE Taylor
takes to the road for
her first headlining
concerts, 2009's
Fearless Tour.

nationally recognizable names, including Jonas. "Hey Stephen," about a "guy I had a crush on," was revealed, not so subtly in the liner notes, to be about Stephen Barker Liles of the country music duo Love and Theft, who she performed with in 2008. She told *The New York Times* in 2008 that "every single one of the guys I've written songs about has been tracked down on MySpace by my fans. I had the opportunity to be more general on this record, but I chose not to. I like to have the last word."

Demonstrating how the ideas flowed out of her, "Love Story," the first single from the album, was written on her bedroom floor in about twenty minutes. With its Romeo and Juliet theme, it combined her love of stories from the past, and fairy-tale imagery, with inspiration taken from her own life—of seeing a boyfriend every day at high school, and then not being able to at all. She imagined giving Shakespeare's tragedy a twist by creating a happy ending, wondering what would happen if there was "a key change" and she turned it "into a marriage proposal."

"... after an entire album of wide-open choruses, it's refreshing to hear Swift tell her story simply. If the melody doesn't stick in your mind, the message at least speaks to the heart."

It was followed by the single "White Horse," which acted as the opposite of the fairy tale of "Love Story." This time, with the realization that there's no knight on a white horse, the romantic fantasy falls apart. The third single from *Fearless* was "You Belong with Me," a song about a dorky teenage girl who feels invisible to the guy she is secretly pining for. This was the character Taylor most aligned with: the girl next door in the periodic table T-shirt, who is so often friend-zoned by her crush.

Taylor was now being pigeonholed as only writing about romantic love. Yet this wasn't quite true. "The Best Day" was a tribute to her family, and in particular her mother, as a thanks for their love and support. She wrote it while touring with Brad Paisley in summer 2007, and as a surprise for Christmas that year, she played it for Andrea, with an edited home video to go alongside it. "She didn't even realize it was me singing until halfway through the song!" Taylor said. "When she finally got it, she just started bawling her eyes out."

Its emotional heart was the nostalgia for childhood, seeing cherished memories like snapshots, and the sadness of growing up too quickly. James Reed of *The Boston Globe* named it the best song on *Fearless*. He wrote, "after an entire album of wide-open choruses, it's refreshing to hear Swift tell her story simply. If the melody doesn't stick in your mind, the message at least speaks to the heart."

Fearless was 2009's best-selling album, spending eleven weeks at No. 1 on the *Billboard* 200 and selling just over 3.2 million copies (in 2017 it would be certified Diamond, with ten million copies sold). When it was named Album of the Year at the Grammys in February 2010, she was, at that time, the youngest recipient of the award.

Taylor took to the road for her first headlining concert tour, the Fearless Tour, in April 2009, where she established her original stage look—the wild curly hair, the minidresses, the cowboy boots, and the friendship bracelets around her wrists, which she would toss out to the crowd as a way of remaining connected. There were 118 shows over fifteen months, and across North America, the UK, Australia, and Japan, the tour grossed $66.5 million.

Taylor had, by this point, decisively crossed over from being a country star into pop culture, and it was her unintentional role in a hugely controversial and cultural moment that had partly shifted her into a new sphere. In September 2009, Taylor was due to perform at the MTV Video Music Awards, where she was also up for an award for the video for "You Belong with Me." Arriving with current boyfriend Taylor Lautner, star of *Twilight* (and her co-star in 2010's *Valentine's Day*), she would have no idea that what later unfolded onstage would cause ripples in her life for many years to come.

ABOVE Closing out a successful year at the Z100's Jingle Ball, Madison Square Garden, New York City, December 11, 2009.

OPPOSITE Taylor brings the Romeo and Juliet theme to life with her performance of "Love Story" during 2009's Fearless Tour.

THE ESSENTIAL... TAYLOR SWIFT

CHAPTER THREE

SPEAK NOW AND RED

PAGE 44 Taylor
Swift's signature
"heart hands" on
the Speak Now
Tour, Milan, Italy,
March 2011.

OPPOSITE A brief
moment of joy
before an infamous
interruption at the
2009 MTV Video
Music Awards.

S tanding on the stage at the MTV Video Music Awards in 2009, like a prom queen in a sparkling silver gown, this was Taylor's moment. She was the first country artist to ever win a VMA, and clutching her "moonman" on the stage, she looked out over the sea of pop, R&B, and hip hop acts. And then, when Kanye West grabbed her mic and declared, "Imma let you finish," her big moment shattered.

Back in her dressing room, she was in tears as her equally emotional mom tried to comfort her; it was like the painful times at school when she was treated as an outsider and rejected by the other girls. She was shortly due to perform "You Belong with Me," where she'd be singing on top of a taxi outside Radio City Music Hall. She pulled herself together, changed into a bright red dress, and threw her all into singing for her life. The next day, the incident made international headline news, and President Obama even weighed in on his disapproval of Kanye's actions.

"I'm not going to say that I wasn't rattled by it, but I had to perform five minutes later, so I had to get back to the place where I could perform," she told daytime talkshow *The View*, as part of an extensive media debrief. Taylor felt burned, but she used the experience, as she always did, to write a song. What she created was a tender ballad called "Innocent," which would appear on her upcoming album, *Speak Now*.

Now that she had been part of a major celebrity feud, there would be further rough patches alongside enormous success. At the Grammys in February 2010, she took home four awards, including Album of the Year for *Fearless*, but she was also criticized for an

off-key duet with Stevie Nicks which meshed "Rhiannon" with "You Belong with Me." She argued against the criticism: "I write songs, and my voice is just a way to get those lyrics across."

For her third album, she would be the sole writer and co-producer for every track. The songs were once again inspired by, and reflective of, her life through 2009 and 2010. The setting of her first two albums had been high school, and now it would cover her world as a young performer, but still with the transience of relationships and the overwhelming ache of lost love. The first single, "Mine," released in August 2010, was an idealized love story narrative about letting her guard down enough to develop a lasting relationship, while wrapping the country pop sound with clever phrasing.

The album, *Speak Now*, followed in October 2010, instantly hitting No. 1 on the *Billboard* 200 with over one million sales. It was the fastest-selling digital album by a female artist, and received widespread praise from critics, including *Rolling Stone*, which named it one of the 50 Best Female Albums of All Time in 2012.

ABOVE After accepting her award for Video of the Year, Beyoncé concedes the stage to Taylor, who makes the acceptance speech that Kanye West prevented her from giving earlier in the evening.

The *Washington Post* described her as the "poet laureate of puberty," while Dolly Parton named her "the greatest thing that's ever happened to country music," and she was ranked by *Forbes* as 2010's seventh-biggest-earning celebrity, with an annual income of $45 million, boosted by endorsements, such as a perfume with Elizabeth Arden, advertising with CoverGirl, and ticket sales for her concerts.

The next singles from the album were "Back to December," "Mean," "The Story of Us," "Sparks Fly," and "Ours." They all touched on the important events in her life, while not naming names (but dropping hints in her liner notes). Her autobiographical songs perfectly suited the internet era, as sleuths pored over the lyrics to find meaning. One blogger worked out that a reference to July 9 in the song "Last Kiss" was about her relationship with Joe Jonas, because she flew to Dallas that day in 2008 to watch him perform.

It was while filming her first movie, *Valentine's Day*, that she met Taylor Lautner, the hot young actor who had become a heartthrob with his role as werewolf Jacob in the *Twilight* franchise. They dated in fall 2009, and she would be inspired to write the lament, "Back to December," where she referenced how he comforted her at the VMAs that infamous September night, and how she regretted having ended it because of her own fear.

> "I'm not going to say that I wasn't rattled by it, but I had to perform five minutes later, so I had to get back to the place where I could perform."

The singer John Mayer would also have a big impact on her—she had dated him when she was nineteen after collaborating on his single "Half of My Heart." "Dear John," with its electric guitar licks and bluesy sound, was a pointed revenge song that reflected the confusion she felt in the push and pull of their relationship. It painted her as a young victim, a girl in a dress crying all the way home after being unable to keep up with his ever-changing rules. It had always been a solace to express herself through music, but now her millions of fans were hanging on every word. "I feel like in my music I can be a rebel," she said. "I can say things I wouldn't say in real life. I couldn't put the sentence together the way I could put the song together."

Through the capital letter hints in her liner notes, "Enchanted" was said to be about a fleeting meeting in New York with Adam Young, of Owl City. "Mean" was a bluegrass rebuke to the bullies who had tried to hold her back, and she also settled scores in "Better than Revenge," about an actress, Camilla Belle, who reportedly stole Joe Jonas from her. It was the most vicious song of her career so far.

In February 2011, she kicked off the Speak Now World Tour in Singapore, and it would finish up in Auckland, New Zealand, the following March. She was truly a global star, with a devoted fan base, and during each concert she further pushed her love of codes and symbols by scrawling on her arm meaningful song lyrics by artists like U2, Tom Petty, Faith Hill, Alanis Morissette, and best friend Selena Gomez.

Her most loyal fans, often wearing sundresses and cowboy boots, were rewarded at each show, when her mother, nicknamed "Mamma Swift," and an assistant would venture into the audience and select the lucky ones to invite backstage. Taylor didn't want the VIP meet-and-greets to be simply for those who paid enough

THE ESSENTIAL... TAYLOR SWIFT

money; rather, they were for those who knew all the words and had
spent hours making their signs.

In "Never Grow Up," she sings about the sad transition from
childhood to adulthood, of being desperate to leave home, but
once in her own apartment in a big city, it's a lonely, colder place.
Taylor had purchased a luxury condo in midtown Nashville in
2009, having once pointed out the apartment block to her mother,
because "it just looked so grown-up." The huge windows provided
a direct view of Music Row, the strip of recording studios and
label offices. She decorated it in a whimsical style, which she
described as "Tim Burton-*Alice in Wonderland*-pirate ship-*Peter
Pan*." There were antique gilded bird cages, a koi pond in the
living room, a topiary rabbit in a marching-band hat, and framed
photos of her family and friends, as well as the moment when
Kanye crashed her acceptance speech, with a handwritten note:
"Life is full of little interruptions."

On tour and in this Nashville apartment, she had already begun
composing new music. With the sense that she needed to evolve,
she was adamant she wanted to move toward a softer pop-rock

sound for what would be her fourth album, *Red*.

Swedish pop magicians Max Martin and Johan "Shellback" Schuster worked on three songs: "We Are Never Ever Getting Back Together," "I Knew You Were Trouble," and "22." They still possessed the classic Swift narrative, the clever phrasing, the heartbreak and joy, but they were far removed from her original country sound. She had begun her career as a teenager with a Tennessee drawl, but had allowed it to soften, alongside the banjos, fiddles, and mandolins which were so prevalent on *Speak Now*. Taylor's look of sparkling dresses, cowboy boots, and a mass of curls would also change, as she cut and straightened her hair, chose leather shorts and blouses and bowler hats, and made red lips her signature.

"We Are Never Ever Getting Back Together," released in August 2012 as the first single from the album, was pure pop. In the studio with Martin and Shellback one day, she expressed her frustration at a relationship where they were continually breaking up and getting back together, and the Swedes encouraged her to develop it as a catchy song. On release it was dismissed by some critics as frivolous, but it was a crossover hit, dominating country radio and pop charts around the world.

The upbeat song was supported by an equally fun music video, where she danced in pajamas and glasses, and with her band dressed as fluffy creatures. In reality, she had the blonde looks of a cheerleader but so often in her songs and videos she was the underdog. Throughout *Red* she took aim at the hipsters—the guy whose indie records are cooler than hers, those who sneer at the mention of her name in "22," and the "Not a lot going on at the moment" T-shirt worn with red heart-shaped glasses in the music video. She was poking fun at, and self-aware of, her own uncoolness at the same time. It may have been laced with

THE ESSENTIAL... TAYLOR SWIFT

the joyousness of a twenty-two-year-old who was "single and happy and carefree and confused and didn't care," but the album came from a place of deep sadness, where she had spent the last Christmas crying over "this earth-shattering . . . absolute crash-and-burn heartbreak."

The only way she could heal was to express it in songwriting, and red, she said, was the color she immediately associated with fast, out-of-control love and loss, which, in the title track, was like a Maserati speeding down a dead-end street. She also used the motif to good effect in "All Too Well," a song about her autumn relationship with Jake Gyllenhaal, whose presence was felt throughout the album.

In a world of raunchiness, Taylor was considered prim and straitlaced—more akin to a princess in a fairy tale than a modern, scantily-clad pop star. For the first time, she hinted in *Red* that she wasn't the good girl people thought she was. On "Treacherous," written with Dan Wilson, she hints that she could be putty in her lover's hands. In "Girl at Home," she resists being the other woman in a cheating man's life, and in "I Knew You Were Trouble," which featured a dubstep bass-drop, the guy in the song takes her to places she's never been. The extended video, where she plays a hipster girl abandoned at a music festival by the bad boy, won the

> **"I feel like in my music I can be a rebel," she said. "I can say things I wouldn't say in real life, I couldn't put the sentence together the way I could put the song together."**

Best Female Video award at the VMAs in 2013. She said in her acceptance speech: "I also want to thank the person who inspired this song, who knows exactly who he is." While it had originally been written about someone else, it was now a missile directed at Harry Styles, who she dated at the end of 2012. At the Grammys the following month, her performance of "We Are Never Ever Getting Back Together" further appeared to reference him, when she put on an English accent for the interlude.

Having made $57 million in 2012, she was one of the best-selling female recording artists in music history, and had a tireless work ethic, as well as "an Oprah-like gift for emotional expressiveness," according to *The New Yorker*, yet she was reduced to being a serial dater. She was incredibly frustrated that her love life was a joke, even when she made her own digs at her penchant for revenge ("So what are you going to do? Did you not Wikipedia me before you called me up?").

At the November 2012 Country Music Association Awards, hosts Carrie Underwood and Brad Paisley made fun of her short-lived romance with Conor Kennedy, which is believed to have inspired "Begin Again," a ballad about a reviving new love. "Are they ever gonna get back together?" Paisley asked. "Like never," replied Carrie. "Maybe she'll write a song about it."

There were similar jokes at the 2013 Golden Globes by the hosts Tina Fey and Amy Poehler, where she was nominated for "Safe and Sound," from *The Hunger Games* soundtrack. Taylor was in the ladies' room at the time, but the auditorium laughed at her expense. She later told *Vanity Fair* that she admired Katie Couric for saying that "There's a special place in hell for women who don't help other women."

Following the release of *Red*, she was now the first female artist, and the fourth artist ever, to have two albums (after *Speak Now*) sell a million copies in their first week. She was also the first female artist to have three consecutive albums hit No. 1 on the *Billboard* 200 for six weeks or more. She embarked on the Red Tour in March 2013, which demonstrated she was a true crowd-pleasing star. She may not have been the best dancer, but, as *The Guardian* commented in its review of the show at London's O2, she was "most at home when she's behind an instrument," and demonstrating true "songcraft."

Even as she was promoting *Red*, she was thinking of her next move, as she confessed that as soon as she put out one album she was "already worried about the next one." And her fifth album would take her to a whole new level of fame.

OPPOSITE Swift is the first solo female artist in 20 years to undertake a national stadium concert tour of Australia, the last being Madonna in 1993.

CHAPTER FOUR

1989

PAGE 58 Taylor
Swift in Manhattan,
New York City,
November 14, 2014.

OPPOSITE Taylor
Swift performs at
the O2 in London
in 2014.

While bringing the Red Tour to venues around the world, Taylor was continually collecting ideas for her fifth album—recording voice memos, noting down lyrics, and playing with ideas for the direction she wanted to take. After *Red* lost out on Album of the Year at the Grammys in 2014, she chose to go for a completely new sound and to signpost this rebirth, it would be influenced and named after the year she was born.

She teamed up again with Max Martin and Shellback, as well as collaborating with producer Jack Antonoff, to fully shift from country to pop, by way of 1980s synths and programmed drums. Her record label, Big Machine, had attempted to persuade her not to make a straight up pop record, and strongly suggested she still include a couple of country songs with their fiddles and banjos.

Even calling the album "1989" was considered a gamble, but she was adamant. She "was really putting my neck on the line, because I was the one saying I need to change directions musically. And my label and management were the ones saying 'Are you sure, are you positive? This is risky.'"

The first single, "Shake It Off," released in August 2014, was an infectious dance-pop number taking aim at the trolls. The pure pop sound, with its cheerleading beat, went straight to No. 1 on the *Billboard* Hot 100, and would earn three Grammy nominations. With her savviness in ensuring her own words weren't exploited, its catchy phrases were some of the first song lyrics to be trademarked.

The accompanying video depicted her as the nerdy girl struggling to keep up with different forms of dancing, yet it also showcased a new look—the sleek blonde bob, and the sundresses and cowboy

THE ESSENTIAL... TAYLOR SWIFT

"[I] was really putting my neck on the line, because I was the one saying I need to change directions musically. And my label and management were the ones saying 'Are you sure, are you positive? This is risky.'"

boots giving way to a more streamlined New York style that would punctuate the next few years.

As well as its familiar themes of love and heartbreak, the album was a celebration of her move to New York. She had been terrified of living there, but once she overcame the fear, she experienced the thrill of being in a city that inspired so many other artists, as expressed in the feel-good opening track of the album, "Welcome to New York."

In an interview with *Rolling Stone* in September 2014, she confessed to being single and loving it. It was during this incarnation that she embraced her famous female friends, and lived the lifestyle akin to that celebrated in her ode to having a good time, "22."

"I really like my life right now," she said. "I have friends around me all the time. I've started painting more. I've been working out a lot. I've started to really take pride in being strong. I love the album I made. I love that I moved to New York. So in terms of being happy, I've never been closer to that."

She may have celebrated being young and free and embracing the heartache with mascara tears in "New Romantics," yet the ghost of her relationship with Harry Styles was present throughout the album, with the tracks "Style" and "Out of the Woods." She was the girl with the red lips and tight little skirt, and he was the boy in the T-shirt and slicked-back hair. In "Wildest Dreams," she goes further than before—remembering his hands in her hair, and his clothes in her room.

The album was a celebration of a woman finding herself after a reckless romance, and this was expressed in the final, and thirteenth,

track, "Clean." Together with "Shake It Off," it was one of the last songs she wrote for the album, conceived when she was in London. Walking out of Liberty department store, she was struck by the realization that someone she used to date had been in the same city for the past two weeks, and she hadn't thought about him at all. She felt that she was finally clean and ready to move on, and the secret message in the liner notes was along the lines of she may have lost him, but she found herself and that means a whole lot more.

Taylor had long felt the misperception of who she was, as played up in the press and in jokes by comedians. So she chose to embrace the role of a serial dater in the satirical "Blank Space," where she acted as the seductive but crazy

girlfriend. "That was the character I felt the media had written for me, and for a long time I felt hurt by it. I took it personally. But as time went by, I realized it was kind of hilarious."

"All You Had to Do Was Stay" came from an embarrassing dream where her ex came to her door and begged her to take him back, and all that she was able to respond was a high-pitched call to stay. "I woke up from the dream, saying the weird part into my phone, figuring I had to include it in something because it was just too strange not to. In pop, it's fun to play around with little weird noises like that."

Above all, she wanted the songs on the album to be addictive. "I am in love with catchy melodies and hooks that are stuck in your head for days, and ideally weeks, and even months," she told *Time* magazine.

Her instincts about the album were right—when *1989* dropped in October 2014, it sold 1.28 million copies in its first week, more than any album in that time period since 2002, and it topped the *Billboard* 200 for eleven non-consecutive weeks, spending the next year in the Top Ten. It also received strong reviews: *Time*

PAGES 64-65 Taylor Swift performs at Dick Clark's New Year's Rockin' Eve, in Times Square on December 31, 2014.

ABOVE Channeling a more streamlined New York style that punctuates the next few years.

THE ESSENTIAL... TAYLOR SWIFT

praised the songs that "fizz and crackle with electricity and self-aware wit," while *Pitchfork* described Swift as having grown up to now inhabit "a fully-realized fantasy of self-reliance, confidence, and ensuing pleasure."

The album was previewed for a select group of fans she had found on Tumblr and on fan blogs, and who she invited for "Secret Sessions" at her homes, where they got the chance to meet her parents, and to try out her home-baking. As part of the deluxe edition she also let listeners in on her creative process by including memos and voicemails to her producer with ideas for her songs. It was a rebuttal of the misogynistic assumption that she wasn't the creative force behind her own work. Given that Ed Sheeran was never questioned as to whether he wrote his

own songs, she said, "we all know it's a feminist issue."

Rolling Stone described *1989* as "The Reinvention of Taylor Swift," and *Time* splashed her on the cover of the November 24, 2014 edition, with the headline, "The Power of Taylor Swift." In December, at the *Billboard* Women in Music event, she accepted the title of Woman of the Year, making her the first artist to win the award twice.

It was the most successful album of her career so far, and with this power, she found a confidence in standing up to music streamers that exploited artists. She had long felt that artists' work was devalued by Spotify, and in November 2014, she took a stand by removing her entire back catalog.

She had previously posted an open letter on her blog to Apple, following its announcement of a three-month free trial for its subscription service, during which time artists would not be compensated. She wrote, "We don't ask you for free iPhones. Please don't ask us to provide you with our music for no compensation." By the end of the day, Apple had reversed the decision, and she was hailed as the savior of struggling musicians.

With the previous pressure she had experienced on her love life, she made the decision to take a break from dating, and to instead cultivate her female friendships. Her home in New York became a gathering place for her celebrity girlfriends, known collectively as the "squad."

The Tribeca townhouse, previously owned by *Lord of the Rings* director Peter Jackson, was as whimsical as her Nashville penthouse. It made appearances on Instagram as she recorded her life with her BFFs and with her cats, Meredith Grey, inspired by *Grey's Anatomy*, and Olivia Benson, after the Mariska Hargitay character in *Law & Order: Special Victims Unit*.

The supermodel Karlie Kloss regularly stayed over in her own guest bedroom, and Taylor had a rack full of white nightgowns so that she and another close friend, Lena Dunham, could dress up as "pioneer women, fresh off the Oregon Trail."

Having turned twenty-five in December 2014, she had truly transitioned from the lanky fifteen-year-old who had dreamed of escaping high school. Now she was living in luxury in the hippest city in the world, with some of the most beautiful, cool women as best friends, including models Cara Delevingne and Gigi Hadid, the singers Selena Gomez and Lorde, and actress Emma Stone. Her millions of followers on Instagram could watch her and Kloss get ready for the Met Gala, or view her baking cookies with Hailee Steinfeld.

As a September 2015 *Vanity Fair* profile described, she "lunches and dines with these girlfriends; she attends concerts with them; she crafts with them; she cooks with them; she walks red carpets with them; many of them appear in pre-taped clips that run during her current world-tour stops; and some of them have even emerged, in the flesh, at her shows, to strut down the stage and wave to the crowd."

When she performed at the Victoria's Secret show in London in December 2014, she looked every inch the glossy-limbed supermodel herself, rather than the geeky girl in glasses who dances on her bed. She now had her own clique that she had not only been accepted into, but was de facto leader. Years later, in the track "You're on Your Own, Kid" from her *Midnights* album, she referenced the pressure she felt during this *1989* period, when she starved her body to be thin, and felt she had to live up to being the perfect host for her Fourth of July parties.

THE ESSENTIAL... TAYLOR SWIFT

It was as if she was enacting revenge on the girls who rejected her when she was at school. It was the same reason she'd purchased a silver Lexus SC 430 convertible, as it was the one driven by Regina George in the 2004 movie *Mean Girls*, who the girls in Pennsylvania idolized.

But there was speculation in social media and in comment pieces as to whether Taylor had turned into a "mean girl" herself, particularly with the release of the music video for "Bad Blood," where she had recruited her famous friends to play girl power assassins. It won Video of the Year and Best Collaboration at the 2015 MTV Video Music Awards, but the song was a barbed attack on another woman. She strongly hinted in an interview with *Rolling Stone* that it was about her feud with Katy Perry, who allegedly poached Taylor's dancers from one of her tours.

In May 2015, she embarked on the 1989 World Tour, which crossed North America, took in dates in Europe, Asia, and Australia, and grossed over $250.7 million. On each stop, she would invite a special guest to perform with her, such as Jennifer Lopez, The Weeknd, Ellie Goulding, Mick Jagger, and even members of her squad, further leading to criticism that she was a name-dropper.

When *1989* won Album of the Year and Best Pop Vocal Album at the 2016 Grammys, she became the first woman to win Album of the Year twice. It was a glorious moment as she was photographed with a blonde bob and an armful of awards, but at the peak of her career, there was destined to be a backlash. During her acceptance speech she made a pointed dig at Kanye West—"to all the young women out there, there are going to be people out there who try to under-cut your success, or take credit for your accomplishments, or your fame."

With them having reunited at the 2015 Grammy Awards, it had appeared as if Taylor and Kanye had made peace. The two were close enough to go for dinner in New York, to chat over phone calls, and she hinted that she'd be open to a collaboration. But then, at the beginning of 2016, in his new track, "Famous," he claimed credit for her success and called her a "bitch." She had become one of the most significant performers of the 2010s, with each of her last three albums selling over one million copies in a week, all the while receiving warm reviews from critics. It was galling that someone would use misogynistic lyrics to take credit. But Kanye and wife Kim Kardashian would retaliate in a move that would be incredibly damaging to her.

> "To all the young women out there, there are going to be people out there who try to under-cut your success, or take credit for your accomplishments, or your fame."

There would also be another celebrity feud over the summer of 2016. Taylor had avoided dating for the past few years, but in March 2015 she began a relationship with Scottish DJ Calvin Harris. They were first seen holding hands at a Kenny Chesney concert in Nashville, and they began showing up in each other's Instagram feeds.

When they split in June 2016, Taylor announced that she had in fact co-written his hit collaboration with Rihanna, "This Is What You Came For," under the pseudonym Nils Sjöberg. Harris lashed out at her revelation. The world Taylor had created around herself, and her reputation, was about to implode.

OPPOSITE TOP Did they make up? Taylor Swift hugs Kanye West after presenting him with the Vanguard Award at the 2015 MTV Video Music Awards in Los Angeles, California.

OPPOSITE BOTTOM LEFT At the 2016 Grammys, Taylor accepts an armful of awards, becoming the first woman to win Album of the Year twice.

OPPOSITE BOTTOM RIGHT Another celebrity feud? This time with ex Calvin Harris, who she had dated from March 2015 to June 2016.

CHAPTER FIVE

REPUTATION

On August 29, 2016, Taylor wrote in her diary, "This summer is the apocalypse." Her eighties-infused album *1989* had stormed the charts, earning critical acclaim and an armful of Grammy awards, and so it was inevitable that there would be a backlash. "I had all the hyenas climb on and take their shots," she later reflected, and these shots felt like continuous bombardment.

There had been too much publicity—following her split with Calvin Harris, she began a very visible relationship with actor Tom Hiddleston, after meeting him at the Met Gala in May 2016. As co-chair of the fashion event, she was the star of the evening, rocking an edgier goth look with a silver snakeskin minidress, bleached hair, and black lips. She had invited her close friends the female rock band Haim to perform, and a video emerged of her and Hiddleston doing a dance-off, at a time when she was still supposedly dating Calvin Harris.

Two weeks after she officially called it quits with Harris, paparazzi photos captured Taylor and Hiddleston kissing on the rocks near her Rhode Island home, and it was splashed on the front page of *The Sun*, with the headline, "Tinker Taylor Snogs a Spy" (referring to his role in the John Le Carré television adaptation *The Night Manager*).

Quickly dubbed "Hiddleswift," they traveled around the world on her private jet, and were snapped holding hands at the Colosseum in Rome. During Fourth of July celebrations with her new best friends Blake Lively and Ryan Reynolds, the actor was pictured frolicking in the waves in an "I heart TS" T-shirt. If people needed a reason to believe Taylor was eager to move on to another relationship, then

this was the evidence, and all the perfect photo-ops seemed too convenient, like they were a massive PR stunt.

That summer, the fallout with Kanye West came to a head following the rapper's release of a disturbing music video for "Famous," where a nude waxwork in Taylor's likeness was in bed with Kanye, his wife Kim Kardashian, and Donald Trump. In July, Kardashian posted on her Snapchat account the recording of a phone call between Taylor and Kanye, where it appeared she had in fact consented to the reference to her in "Famous." It painted Taylor as a liar who had played the victim.

On July 17, World Snake Day, Kim further twisted the knife, when she tweeted: "They have holidays for everybody, I mean everything these days," and her fans headed straight to Taylor's Instagram, where they bombarded her with snake emojis.

Taylor released a statement over the leaked call, stating she would "very much like to be excluded from this narrative"—words that would come back to haunt her. With #Taylorswiftisoverparty trending on Twitter, and gossip blogs and magazines speculating on her cancellation, she retreated completely from public view.

After her split from Hiddleston, she had quietly begun dating the British actor Joe Alwyn, and as she divided her time between New York and his hometown of London, she ensured she kept the relationship completely private.

"You have a fully manufactured frame job, in an illegally recorded phone call, which Kim Kardashian edited and then put out to say to everyone that I was a liar," she said in a 2023 interview with *Time*. "That took me down psychologically to a place I've never been before. I moved to a foreign country. I didn't leave a rental house for a year. I was afraid to get on phone calls. I pushed away most people in my life because I didn't trust anyone anymore. I went down really, really hard."

In August 2017, fans were quick to notice that she had wiped all previous posts from her social media accounts. Just a few days later, she posted to Instagram a set of three videos of CGI snakes, and it was followed by the announcement that there would be a new album coming on November 10.

Having experienced a "career death," all she could do was rise again, and this time she was taking back the power. The snake emoji had been used as a mass form of bullying, and now she was owning it as the leading motif for her new visuals.

> "I moved to a foreign country. I didn't leave a rental house for a year. I pushed away most people in my life because I didn't trust anyone anymore. I went down really, really hard."

The first single from the album, "Look What You Made Me Do," was released on August 25, and it immediately set the tone. With its melodramatic strings and piano, and pounding electronic drumbeats, it was an angry revenge piece that took aim at those who had

attacked her. It also showed a new, vengeful Taylor telling someone on the phone that the old version of Taylor Swift was dead.

The song was about many things at once: of being called a snake, her feud with Kanye West and Katy Perry, the social media take-down. The accompanying video was loaded with references from her past to pick over. She first crawls zombie-like out of a grave marked "Here Lies Taylor Swift's Reputation," and stands beside another headstone marked "Nils Sjoberg." Later, she is surrounded by snakes and bedecked with snake jewelry; there is a giant birdcage, like the one in her Nashville apartment; and there is a thinly veiled impression of Katy Perry with her *Witness*-era short, bleached hair.

All her previous incarnations—the Taylor with the fringed dress, boots, and guitar, the one in nerdy glasses and a T-shirt scrawled with the names of her friends, and the one who says, "I would very much like to be excluded from this narrative"—are mocked and killed off by her new, deadlier identity.

As Caryn Ganz described in *The New York Times*, "Look What You Made Me Do" was "fury, it's vengeance, it's gossip. It's a horror movie, a fairy tale contorted into a calamity . . . This song is for the

THE ESSENTIAL... TAYLOR SWIFT

OPPOSITE She's
back! Taylor Swift
comes out fighting
on the opening
night of her 2018
Reputation Tour.

base—the superfans on the internet who are always ready for a fight."

In one moment in the video, as she lies in a bath filled with jewels, there is a glimpse of a one-dollar bill. Over the summer of 2016, she had also been preparing her testimony for a court case against radio DJ David Mueller, who had been fired three years before when she reported him for putting his hand up her skirt while they posed for a photograph backstage. After he sued her for defamation, she countersued, for just $1 in damages. When it came to court in August 2017, she was ready to fight, and she refused to be bullied as she gave evidence. She won the case, and she was hailed for making an important stand against sexual harassment.

In an interview with *Time* in 2023, she described *Reputation* as "a goth-punk moment of female rage at being gaslit by an entire social structure." Although it had revealing love songs that offered insight into the crazy summer of 2016 and the romance that saved her, it was also a "complete defense mechanism."

The album artwork was black and white, like the newspaper print that had tormented her over the last year, and in the lead-up to the album's release, she avoided publicity and interviews, only sharing news and updates on social media, as a way of controlling her own narrative and allowing the music to speak for itself.

She made an exception for *Saturday Night Live*, appearing as the musical guest on November 11, where she debuted the second single from the album, ". . .Ready for It?" Performing as a goth against a black background flooded with red lights, and clutching a microphone wrapped with a jeweled snake, it was a swaggering, angry, and suggestive performance—the most dramatic switch she had ever made in her ten-year career. *1989* had remade her as a pop star, but this new sound was jaw-dropping with its mixture of electronica, hip hop, and industrial goth, exploring the dangers of stardom.

If she had made a career of feeding her fans clues through the lyrics and liner notes, then the speculation around the subject and meaning of her songs went into overdrive. As well as the Easter eggs in her music videos, each track was loaded with references as to what her life had been like over the last year.

In "End Game," featuring Future and Ed Sheeran, she dipped into hip hop with the chorus. She was the unapologetic playgirl who teases the narcissists, flies them around the world, and then takes pleasure in leaving them before they can hurt her, in "I Did Something Bad." Similarly, in "Getaway Car" she uses the imagery of a heist as a metaphor for her short-lived rebound romance with Tom Hiddleston—it was doomed from the start—and in "This Is Why We Can't Have Nice Things", a sneering and bratty shot at her enemies, she laughs at the notion of forgiveness.

It wasn't all pointed revenge and bombastic surface—there were softer tracks that gave an insight into her low-key relationship with actor Joe Alwyn, who she began dating in late 2016 after months of friendship. "Don't Blame Me" was an electro-pop gospel to addictive, crazy love. "Dress" was not only one of the raciest of her career, but hinted at when they first met. With his buzzcut and her bleached hair, it was a clear reference to their looks at the 2016 Met Gala.

ABOVE & OPPOSITE TOP Taking back the power. The snake, previously used as a way of shaming Taylor, is a leading motif for her new stage visuals.

OPPOSITE BOTTOM A break from the gothic aesthetics and the snake imagery with a rainbow-hued interlude as she performs "Shake It Off" with Charli XCX and Camila Cabello.

There were secret meetings in dive bars late at night, as memorialized in "Delicate," and in the video, a necklace with the initial "J." At a time when her reputation was at its worst, she sings that he must like her for who she really is. Yet she worries about whether she's too quick to reveal herself to him.

"Gorgeous" imagines an instant infatuation with a guy with ocean-blue eyes and an accent she makes fun of—a recurring theme for future tracks about Joe—and where she curses herself for going home to her cats instead of declaring her feelings.

In "Call It What You Want" she reflects on her hibernation after her world imploded. The drama queens may take swings, but she feels protected by her lover who she trusts and who she asks to run away with her. The final track on the album, "New Year's Day," was a sweetly melancholic piano ballad about holding on to the memories while cleaning up the bottles and glitter after midnight.

THE ESSENTIAL... TAYLOR SWIFT

THE ESSENTIAL... TAYLOR SWIFT

Reputation sold one million copies the week it was released, making it the highest-selling album of 2017. Her song for Little Big Town, "Better Man," won the Country Music Association award for Song of the Year, and she was featured on *Time*'s Person of the Year cover as a "silence breaker" for her victory in her sexual assault trial.

She had come back fighting, but still, she was criticized for her ambivalent stance following Donald Trump's tumultuous November 2016 defeat of Hillary Clinton. She hadn't endorsed either candidate, and rather than attending the Women's March in January, she had only tweeted her support. How to come out politically, and to reveal her allyship with the LGBTQ+ community, was something she would think hard about while she embarked on the Reputation Stadium Tour.

As her first all-stadium tour, it was high-tech, brash, and dramatic, with pyrotechnics and video projection, but in the middle of the set, she took a break from the gothic aesthetics and snake imagery with a technicolor interlude as she performed "Delicate." Now wearing a rainbow-striped minidress, she spoke to the audience, their lit-up bracelets transforming them into a sparkling sea, of the value of finding something real amidst gossip and rumor.

The rainbow joyousness continued with colorful confetti falling during "Shake It Off," and following this interlude, she was back in glittering black, but this time more introspective for an acoustic performance of "Dancing with Our Hands Tied."

> **"I was looking out at the faces of the people who helped me get back up. I'll never forget the ones who stuck around."**

The Reputation Stadium Tour broke the record for the highest-grossing American tour, and for Taylor, the most emotional part "was knowing I was looking out at the faces of the people who helped me get back up. I'll never forget the ones who stuck around." By the time she had finished the tour in Tokyo in November 2018, she was ready to find peace in new music, and to finally speak out about the issues she cared about.

CHAPTER SIX

LOVER

OPPOSITE A
powder blue coat,
worn to the Vogue
BAFTA party with
Joe Alwyn in early
2019, suggests a
softer, more hopeful
direction for Taylor.

PAGE 88 At the
2019 American
Music Awards.

I f *Reputation* was a gothic revenge fantasy, where all Taylor's darkest thoughts were unleashed within its gritty black, white, and red color scheme, then her next album would be a complete about-turn.

While a clear fan favorite, *Reputation* hadn't been as well received as previous albums. It had sold 4.5 million copies in comparison to *1989*'s ten million and was snubbed at the Grammys. She was introspective—"I just need to make a better record"—and tonally and aesthetically, her new music would be a metamorphosis. Not only was it the first album produced under a new record deal with Universal Music Group, and which she had full ownership of, but it was written at a time when she felt like she "could take a full deep breath again." She worked with collaborators Jack Antonoff, Annie Clark (known as St. Vincent), Joel Little, and The Dixie Chicks to hone this softer, more hopeful direction.

She would offer further clues to its mood in her wardrobe choices—arriving at the *Vogue* BAFTA party with Joe Alwyn in a powder blue wrap coat, and at the iHeartRadio Music Awards, in March 2019 in L.A., in a rainbow sequined playsuit and with heels decorated with butterflies.

The first hint that there was new music coming was an Instagram post on April 13 of a pastel background with a clock counting down to thirteen days. It was followed by further teasers—including a pair of hands with pastel nails and a love heart made from diamonds.

Finally, on April 26, she held a photo call in Nashville, where she posed against a butterfly wing mural in a powder blue skirt and top, with pink tips in her hair. She had personally commissioned

THE ESSENTIAL... TAYLOR SWIFT

the mural from street artist Kelsey Montague, and it announced the release of a new single, "Me!," a duet with Brendon Urie from Panic! at the Disco.

This new, bubble-gum-sweet single just screamed upbeat fun. There was a marching band drumbeat, a catchy chorus, and the video was laced with Easter eggs to treat her fans. It opens with a snake transforming into butterflies, a clear metaphor for the light bursting from the darkness of the *Reputation* era,

OPPOSITE & ABOVE
A rainbow-sequined playsuit and heels decorated with butterflies at the iHeartRadio Music Awards in March 2019 offer more hints to Taylor's new direction

and then breaks into a joyous, pastel world—as if it's the land of Oz awakened from a curse. In one scene in the video, as she sits on a large unicorn gargoyle, she looks out on a cityscape with a pink neon sign saying "Lover."

It would be a signpost to the name of her seventh studio album, which she announced on Instagram Live on June 13, with a release date, August 23, adding up to 13 (8 + 2 + 3).

She also revealed that the next single, "You Need to Calm Down," would be released at midnight, with the music video premiering on *Good Morning America* a few days later. As a song that takes aim at internet trolls and homophobia, it was a clear marker of her stance on LGBTQ+ rights.

The video was bursting with technicolor campness, as Taylor played the bikini-clad queen of a rainbow trailer park, and with cameos from queer stars of *Drag Race* and *Queer Eye*. One moment saw pop star Hayley Kiyoko aim a bow and arrow at a target with the number five—a clue that the next single revealed would be "The Archer," the album's fifth track—and Ellen DeGeneres receives a "Cruel Summer" tattoo from Queen singer Adam Lambert, referring to the third single from the album. It ended with a call to sign a petition to support the Equality Act, to prohibit gender- and sex-based discrimination in the US. Taylor was now ready to bring her political stance to the fore.

She had been accused of sidestepping the important political issues of the day, leading some to question what side of the political spectrum she was on. She was dragged for being silent during the presidential election, but it was exactly what she had been taught as a young female artist. The Dixie Chicks became pariahs overnight after making a stand against George Bush and the Iraq War. Now that she had left her original label, Big Machine, after six albums, she felt more confident in being able to express her support for the issues that mattered to her.

Lover would be her most optimistically romantic album so far. As she described to *Vogue*, it felt like a new beginning, and was "really a love letter to love, in all of its maddening, passionate, exciting, enchanting, horrific, tragic, wonderful glory." Over the eighteen tracks, she paid tribute to her great loves—her boyfriend and her mother, and the places that had shaped her, including New York's West Village and her new life in London.

As a way of offering a further confessional insight into her life, the deluxe editions of the album included scanned entries from the diaries she'd kept from the age of thirteen.

"There is an element to my fanbase where we feel like we grew up together. I'll be going through something, write the album about it, and then it'll come out, and sometimes it'll just coincide with what they're going through. Kind of like they're reading my diary," she said. She also continued her tradition of holding "Secret Sessions" over the summer to give her closest fans a first listen to the album.

The upbeat opening track, "I Forgot That You Existed," with its jaunty piano, was an announcement that she was over the *Reputation*-era feuds. She insists she's stopped thinking about the person that wronged her—she doesn't feel love or hate, just indifference, and she was truly over the pain, or was she? In "Cruel Summer," co-produced by Jack Antonoff and St. Vincent's Annie Clark, she appeared to be writing about the painful summer of 2016.

Much of the album was about her relationship with Joe Alwyn, for whom she had upped sticks and escaped to London. In the track "London Boy," she lists all the things she loves about the city, from exploring Camden Market and Hampstead Heath, to watching rugby in the pub with his best mates from uni, and with the odd phrase lifted from her British friends.

OPPOSITE With Brendon Urie of Panic! at the Disco fame performing their duet "Me!" at the 2019 Billboard Music Awards.

THE ESSENTIAL... TAYLOR SWIFT

"There is an element to my fanbase where we feel like we grew up together. I'll be going through something, write the album about it... and sometimes it'll just coincide with what they're going through. Kind of like they're reading my diary."

The dreamy "Lover," with its stirring orchestra, was the song she was most proud of, as it idealized the ordinariness of finding a soul mate, where new rules could be created. In a *New York Times* video feature, "Diary of a Song," she revealed the idea had come to her in the middle of the night like a "glittery cloud" of inspiration as she imagined the last two people on a dancefloor, swaying together and wondering how long they have know each other; is it seconds or years?

"Cornelia Street" was one of the most analyzed tracks on the album, offering a tantalizing glimpse into her love story. In reality, Taylor had rented an apartment on Cornelia Street, in Greenwich Village, and here, in the back of a cab after a drunken night, she offers to take someone home. She's so infatuated that she could never return to this street if it falls apart.

There was "Death by a Thousand Cuts," its upbeat sound contrasting with the downbeat lyrics, where alcohol isn't enough to dull the pain of a break-up. If "Lover" was about all the mundane tasks of setting up an idealized home filled with romance, then in this version, the windows of the house are boarded up. "False God" features sultry saxophones and offers a worship of the sensual as she laments the frustrations of a transatlantic relationship, and the song shares the religious metaphors of "Cornelia Street."

As much as she glorified her romance, which had lasted three years, she would ensure the revelations were only contained within her lyrics—she was determined to retain her privacy, and so Joe was not up for discussion in interviews. "That's where the

THE ESSENTIAL... TAYLOR SWIFT

boundary is, and that's where my life has become manageable," she told *The Guardian* in August 2019.

The album wasn't all about romantic love. "Soon You'll Get Better," a country ballad with The Dixie Chicks providing banjo, fiddles, and backing vocals, revealed her mother's cancer battle and the endless stays in hospital. The anthemic "The Man" lectured on the double standards where Leonardo DiCaprio is praised for his playboy image, whereas a woman can never get away with even minor transgressions.

The final track on the album, "Daylight," revealed her growth since *Red*, where she realizes that rather than burning red, love can be golden. It was a mature reflection on the damage over the last few years, of the cruelty of a harsh city where she became a joke, and trusted the wrong people, and how this new love she found was an awakening.

One of the most melodramatic tracks on the album, "Miss Americana and the Heartbreak Prince," as atmospheric as Lana Del Rey, used a high school setting as a metaphor for how she had grown up as an unquestioning patriot, but could now see

PAGE 98-99 June 1, 2019, California, US. Taylor Swift performs at iHeartRadio Wango Tango.

ABOVE Boo Hiss! Scott Borchetta (L) and Scooter Braun. Borchetta refuses Swift the chance to buy back her masters when he sells his record label Big Machine to Braun, an ally of Kanye West.

ABOVE A live performance on ABC's *Good Morning America* on August 22, 2019 to promote *Lover* is also where Taylor announces her intention to re-record her earlier albums.

the dangers of the type of nationalism that Donald Trump was espousing.

She further made her politics clear when she chose to endorse Phil Bredesen, the Democratic Tennessee candidate in the November 2018 Senate race. Her intervention led to a huge spike in voter registrations, as she appealed to young people to make sure their voices were heard.

In the documentary *Miss Americana*, which was filmed during the Reputation Tour, she revealed how she grappled with her decision to speak up about the issues that she cared about. Her dad was worried for her safety, but she was insistent. "I've educated myself now, and it's time to take the masking tape off my mouth, like, forever."

Lover was the top-selling album of 2019, praised by critics for its optimistic beats and a narrative that refused to stick to one sound, and it would go on to earn three Grammy nominations, including Song of the Year for the title track. At the same time as she was promoting its themes of transformational love, she was entering into a new battle with powerful figures.

Taylor had been her record label Big Machine's biggest act, but the new deals with Universal, and then Republic Records, not only gave her more agency over her own work, but a clause in her contract stated that UMG would share proceeds of its Spotify equity with all its artists.

After the release of *Lover*, Scott Borchetta put Big Machine up for sale, and when Taylor asked if she could buy back the original recordings, or masters, for her previous six albums, he turned her down. She was devastated to discover her back catalog was sold to Scooter Braun's Ithaca Holdings as part of a $140 million deal. Braun was an ally of Kanye West, and she wondered what nefarious plans he might have for her music. She wrote on Tumblr that it was her "worst case scenario." Taylor's frankness about the painful situation of not owning her music opened a discussion around why musicians didn't necessarily have rights to their own masters.

> "I've educated myself now, and it's time to take the masking tape off my mouth, like, forever."

THE ESSENTIAL... TAYLOR SWIFT

FAR LEFT Showing some girl power with Camila Cabello (L) and Halsey (R) as they perform "Shake It Off."

LEFT Making history. Taylor wins six awards at the AMAs, taking her career total to 29, surpassing Michael Jackson's record of 24.

In August, live on *Good Morning America* as she promoted *Lover*, she announced her plan to re-record her albums, starting in November 2020, when she would be contractually able to. At first it seemed like an impossibly huge task, but she was driven by the outrage and anger she felt at "having my life's work taken away from me by someone who hates me."

Named as Artist of the Decade, she opened the 2019 American Music Awards standing against a black background, wearing a plain white shirt printed with the names of the six albums for which she didn't own the rights. On the back of the shirt was "Fearless," and after opening with the clapback against misogyny "The Man," she performed a medley of her greatest hits—a strong statement that she was reclaiming what was hers.

In the final song on the album, "Daylight," the closing words about her desire to be known by acts of love and not hate were prescient on her need to take control of her own music.

CHAPTER SEVEN
THE FOLK ERA

In one moment in her *Miss Americana* documentary, Taylor reflects on the significance of turning thirty. Now in a happier place after a tumultuous few years, she wanted to enjoy her fame and good grace while she still could, as she was well aware that female artists had a shelf life. She also thought endlessly about how her sound should evolve in this next decade.

She penned a piece for *Elle*'s April 2019 edition—"30 Things I Learned Before Turning 30"—where she described how she learned "to stop hating every ounce of fat on my body. I worked hard to retrain my brain that a little extra weight means curves, shinier hair, and more energy," and how to make cocktails "like Pimm's cups, Aperol spritzes, Old-Fashioneds, and Mojitos because . . . 2016." If she thought that year was dramatic, she would need a whole new repertoire of cocktails for 2020.

Having been cast as Bombalurina in Andrew Lloyd Webber's *Cats*, the movie bombed on its release in December 2019. Her original song "Beautiful Ghosts," however, was nominated for a Golden Globe, and she attended the January 2020 ceremony with Joe Alwyn. Later that month, *Miss Americana* was shown at the opening night gala for the Sundance Film Festival, before being streamed on Netflix.

As for taking *Lover* on the road, she mapped out a simplified tour, with four stadium events in America, and a tour of the European festival circuit, which would have included headlining Glastonbury. Following the COVID-19 outbreak in March, and with international borders shutting down, all her dates for the year were cancelled. As stay-at-home orders were put in place, she

THE ESSENTIAL... TAYLOR SWIFT

"I worked hard to retrain my brain that a little extra weight means curves, shinier hair, and more energy."

OPPOSITE
Sweeping in for another award nomination at the 2020 Golden Globes.

rented a home in London with Joe and her three cats, Meredith, Olivia, and Benjamin.

Taylor's lockdown was much like everyone else's who was kept at home. She cooked, drank wine on the sofa while watching old films she'd never seen before, and chatted to friends and family over Zoom. She also wanted to do what she could to help, and she sent money to fans who were struggling with unemployment at the time.

"I think right now we have to connect with our humanity more than we ever have before," she said during a presenting slot on SiriusXM. "So, that's one thing that I've been loving seeing is outreach, people being there for each other in this time."

On April 27, 2020, she posted an image on social media with a caption, "Not a lot going on at the moment," but it turned out that between Instagramming her cats, she'd been busy working on new music. With just seventeen hours' notice, Taylor Swift announced a surprise quarantine album, *Folklore*.

"Most of the things I had planned this summer didn't end up happening, but there is something I hadn't planned on that DID happen," she wrote on Instagram. "I'll be releasing my entire brand new album of songs I've poured all of my whims, dreams, fears, and musings into."

She recorded the music in isolation, setting up a studio in the spare bedroom, and collaborating with her "musical heroes" remotely. These included Jack Antonoff, "basically musical family at this point," The National's Aaron Dessner, who provided keys and piano, his brother Bryce, who developed string arrangements, Justin Vernon of Bon Iver, and William Bowery, the pseudonym of Joe Alwyn.

The album came with a series of folksy black and white images by Beth Garrabrant of Taylor surrounded by forest. It not only reflected the nostalgic, alternative sound that was aligned with cottagecore aesthetics, but also of living through a pandemic, when the only way of connecting to people and the world was by going for walks in parks and woodland.

Earning a Guinness World Record for the most opening-day streams of an album by a female artist, *Folklore* was instantly critically acclaimed, with *The Guardian* giving it five stars and *Rolling Stone* describing it as her greatest album, so far. The biographical details of previous albums had been manna to her fans, but they also allowed for her to be satirized for her feuds and love affairs. This time, Taylor's songwriting took center stage, and there was now no doubt about her talents. She found this freeing because it existed "on its own merit without thinking, 'oh, people are listening to this because it tells them something that you could read in a tabloid.' It feels like a completely different experience."

The tracks were folksy, gentle, and intimate—more indie than radio-friendly pop. She used the full breadth of her songwriting

From Emmy® Winning Director LANA WILSON and Academy Award® Winning Filmmakers Behind 20 FEET FROM STARDOM

sundance

A NETFLIX ORIGINAL DOCUMENTARY

Miss Americana

IN SELECT THEATERS AND ON   TAYLOR SWIFT

NETFLIX | JAN 31

ABOVE *Miss Americana* is streamed on Netflix at the end of January 2020

skills to explore fictional worlds and characters, while also developing her own universe that used reoccurring references in different tracks. As she said of the music, "The lines between fantasy and reality blur and the boundaries between truth and fiction become almost indiscernible." Given that she'd spent her lockdown absorbing literature and movies, references peppered the lyrics— from *Peter Pan* and *The Great Gatsby* in the first track on the album, "The One," to the running metaphor of life as a movie.

There were three songs on the album—"Cardigan," "Betty," and "August" that when taken together told the story of a teenage love triangle, through all three characters' perspectives. In "Cardigan," the narrator, Betty, using the image of a cardigan that still holds on to its scent twenty years later, looks back on an intense relationship from years before, where her lover, James, cheated on her. At the same time as this fictional world, the symbolism in the song was reminiscent of "Cornelia Street" and "Delicate" in its exploration of a hot love affair in New York.

"Betty," a nod to country with its harmonica, is narrated from the perspective of James, where he reveals he ditched Betty after a school dance. As he's walking home, the other girl arrives in her car and tempts him for a summer fling. James begs Betty's forgiveness saying that at seventeen years old he is young and inexperienced. Coming from the perspective of the other girl, "August" reveals her infatuation during this summer affair, as she lives in hope that they could be a real couple beyond the summer months.

In the sweeping "The Last Great American Dynasty," she tells the story of eccentric heiress Rebekah Harkness, the previous owner of her Rhode Island house, and she draws parallels with her own life. Another biographical song, "Epiphany," the thirteenth

CHAPTER SEVEN THE FOLK ERA   113

track, was about her grandfather Dean, who fought on the island of Guadalcanal in 1942.

"My Tears Ricochet," the first song she conceived, and the one she considered the saddest on the album, alludes to a devastating divorce. With its theme of karma and betrayals, she thought of the superhero stories where the hero's biggest nemesis is the best friend turned villain.

As soon as Aaron Dessner sent her an ominous piano sample, she was inspired to write "Mad Woman," about female rage and gaslighting and the story of a "misfit widow getting gleeful revenge," and where the reference to witches harks back to "I Did Something Bad."

Many of the tracks had "lyrical parallels." In "This Is Me Trying," the narrator, struggling in a life crisis, drives to an overlook to contemplate ending it all, as does the narrator of "Hoax." The painful yearning for lost love is conveyed through metaphors involving movie scenes and unhappy endings.

There was an overarching theme of the pressures of fame. In "Mirrorball," the reflective, glittering surface of a disco ball is also broken into a million pieces, and in "Peace," she conveys her desire to lead a normal life, despite the intense scrutiny.

As with "Peace," "Invisible String" appeared to reference her relationship with Joe, using the metaphor of his love as a golden thread that pulled her towards the peace of her *Lover* era. The final song on the album, "Hoax," dealt with a similar theme as she speaks of leaving a part of herself in New York, where she still feels the pain in her scars, from the intense public scrutiny.

There was also a bonus track, "The Lakes," which was inspired by a trip to the Lake District. Just like the romantic poets who retreated there, she imagines her own escape from the online trolls to a place filled with romanticism and light-filled night skies, as long as her muse is right beside her. This muse was Joe Alwyn, and

during lockdown, as she heard him compose music on the piano, they formed part of the tracks "Betty" and "Exile."

On Sunday, November 22, she posted a black and white photo on a couch in the wooden cabin, again using the caption "not a lot going on at the moment." There was huge speculation as to what it could mean—was she about to drop a music video for "Exile," or to announce one of her re-records? The surprise was the release of *Folklore: The Long Pond Studio Sessions*, both as an album and an intimate concert documentary film on Disney+. In September, she and her collaborators Jack Antonoff and Aaron Dessner had met in person at Long Pond Studio, an isolated wood cabin in upstate New York, to record a live session of *Folklore*.

The film offered a new intimacy in seeing Taylor in such a stripped-back setting, absolutely in her element with her fellow musicians, and where the interiors of the cabin and the woodland setting reinforced the wistful sound.

Further, it turned out that she was about to drop more music, making the announcement on December 10 that *Evermore*, the "sister album" to *Folklore*, was coming out at midnight.

"To put it plainly, we just couldn't stop writing songs," she wrote. "To try and put it more poetically, it feels like we were standing on the edge of the folklorian woods and had a choice: to turn and go back or to travel further into the forest of this music. We chose to wander deeper in."

The new cover art, which focused on her long-plaited hair and plaid coat as she faces toward woodland, harked back to the autumnal mood of "All Too Well." The songs, while still folksy, were more buoyant. The picked guitars of opening track and lead single "Willow" set the mood for the album, and in its music video, a cardigan-clad Taylor follows a golden string into a magical kingdom, where she's a witch casting love spells in a forest. It may have been cozy cottagecore, but it still had some killer lines.

There was a return to her country origins with "Cowboy like Me," and "No Body, No Crime" with Haim, which both referred to fictional crimes. The former, featuring Marcus Mumford on backing vocals, was, as Taylor described, about "two young con artists who fall in love while hanging out at fancy resorts trying to score rich romantic beneficiaries."

"No Body, No Crime" appeared to be partnered with "Tolerate It" as part of her self-described "'unhappily ever after' anthology of marriages gone bad that includes infidelity, ambivalent toleration, and even murder."

Another pairing was the two songs about Dorothea, "the girl who left her small town to chase down Hollywood dreams," and which, like "Betty," was written from a male perspective. We hear Dorothea's point of view in "'Tis the Damn Season," as she returns home for the holidays and rekindles an old flame.

There were upbeat tracks like "Gold Rush," where she eulogizes his ocean eyes, the golden hair falling into place like dominoes, and her jealousy that others are after him—a feeling also expressed in "Lover," where she feels suspicious that everyone who sees him wants him.

For all those who felt aggrieved by the way a relationship ended, "Closure" was a refusal to be soothed after being so casually dismissed as a problem that needs solving.

> "We just couldn't stop writing songs. It feels like we were standing on the edge of the folklorian woods and had a choice: to turn and go back or to travel further into the forest of this music. We chose to wander deeper in."

On *Folklore*, the thirteenth track was about her grandfather, and on *Evermore*, it was a tribute to her opera-singer grandmother Marjorie Finlay, where she conveys her regret at not asking her all about her life when she was alive, but whose presence she feels around her now.

At the same time as *Evermore* was storming the charts, she embarked on the process of re-recording her old albums. By placing "Taylor's Version" in brackets after the title, and by including tracks from the "vault," it would ensure that listeners would be attracted to these new releases—it was something that no artist had ever attempted on such a scale. Further, in February 2021, she became the first woman to win Album of the Year at the Grammys, when *Folklore* scooped the title. The following year, *Evermore* would also be nominated. This folk era would be an important element in her journey to becoming one of the most successful musicians of all time.

ABOVE LEFT
Showcasing her folk era style, Taylor Swift performs onstage at the 2021 Grammy Awards.

ABOVE RIGHT
With musical collaborators Jack Antonoff (L) and Aaron Dessner (R).

OPPOSITE & PAGE 120-121 Taylor Swift makes history again, winning Album of the Year at the 2021 Grammys, the first woman to do so.

THE ESSENTIAL... TAYLOR SWIFT

CHAPTER EIGHT

MIDNIGHTS
AND THE
RE-RECORDS

On February 11, 2021, Taylor appeared on *Good Morning America* to announce the upcoming release of *Fearless (Taylor's Version)*. She also revealed it would include never-released vault tracks to give fans the "full picture" of the album. The re-recordings were not supposed to be new interpretations, but "the same but better," to devalue the original albums that she had no control over.

Rather than starting in chronological order, she began with her second album, it was stronger than her debut, launched her as a global star with the Grammy for Album of the Year, and it included some of her most iconic hits and melodies. Now in her thirties, she was singing the lyrics she wrote as a teenager, but revisiting them as an adult gave them a universal quality, as if they could speak to all ages.

She went in "line by line" to "listen to every single vocal and think, you know, what are my inflections here. If I can improve upon it, I did. But I really did want this to be very true to what I initially thought of and what I had initially written. But better. Obviously."

Her voice had matured over the years. As well as having dropped the Nashville twang somewhere between *Speak Now* and *1989*, she had evened out the weaknesses in her pitch control. The differences in the re-recorded tracks were barely noticeable—the odd tweak of sharpening and greater clarity.

As *Pitchfork* described it: "These versions are slightly more polished, like photos touched up on Instagram with a press of a button: The sound is brighter, the mix is clearer, each peal of guitar is sharper."

As well as including "Today Was a Fairytale," a single she had released to coincide with her role in the movie *Valentine's Day*, there

were six new songs on the album which were recorded with Jack Antonoff and Aaron Dessner. In tribute to her Nashville roots, she dueted with Maren Morris on "You All Over Me," and recruited Keith Urban to feature on two "From the Vault" ballads, "That's When" and "We Were Happy."

In "Mr. Perfectly Fine," seemingly an extension of "Forever and Always" in its chastising of a man who changes his mind, she reveals a phrase that would become indelible in Taylor lore, when she describes an ex as being self-centered and heedlessly cruel. This phrase became an important touchpoint for "All Too Well." Listening back to the unreleased vault tracks, it revealed insight into how she kept phrases and melodies in mind, or how she had originally scrapped one track from the album in favor of another.

On its release, *Fearless (Taylor's Version)* became the only re-recorded album to ever top the charts, and it also made her the first female artist to have three No. 1 albums in less than a year—after *Folklore* in July 2020 and *Evermore* in December 2020. It also had the biggest first-day album debut of 2021 on Spotify, with over fifty million streams.

ABOVE Backstage at the 2021 Rock & Roll Hall of Fame induction ceremony for Carole King (second right). Also pictured are Keith Urban, who Taylor recruited for two "From the Vault" tracks, and Nicole Kidman.

THE ESSENTIAL... TAYLOR SWIFT

Will Hodgkinson, in his review for *The Times*, described it as "wholesome as apple pie" and "a nostalgic return to Swift's coming of age, just before she became one of the biggest singers in the world."

Two months after *Fearless (Taylor's Version)* debuted at No. 1 on the *Billboard* 200 chart, she announced its follow-up—*Red (Taylor's Version)*. "This will be the first time you hear all 30 songs that were meant to go on *Red*," she told her followers on social media. "And hey, one of them is even ten minutes long."

The revelation that there was a ten-minute version of "All Too Well" only added to the anticipation and excitement at the album's imminent release. She described how the album "resembled a heartbroken person. It was all over the place, a fractured mosaic of feelings that somehow all fit together in the end. Happy, free, confused, lonely, devastated, euphoric, wild, and tortured by memories past."

Like *Fearless (Taylor's Version)*, this second re-release was faithful to the original, bringing back the collaborations with Gary Lightbody and Ed Sheeran, and replicating every distinction, including the giggle and the exclamation at the wrap of "Stay Stay Stay."

OPPOSITE With Ed
Sheeran, a longtime
collaborator of
Taylor Swift's, and
who features on
two tracks on *Red*
(Taylor's Version).

The extended version of "All Too Well" is a further punch at a
relationship that had such a visceral effect on her as she was writing
Red. It flowed with pain and confusion, making digs at his tendency
for younger girlfriends, the way he regaled her father with stories, like
he was on a late-night talk show, and the heartbreak she felt when he
failed to show for her twenty-first birthday party.

The ten-minute song was accompanied by a short film, written and
directed by Taylor, and which cast Sadie Sink as the besotted twenty-
one-year-old who goes through her "first catastrophic, cataclysmic
heartbreak," and Dylan O'Brien as the older man who breaks her
heart. Having always plotted out her music videos, Taylor had
transitioned into full control as director, further fulfilling her desire for
giving a complete picture when telling stories.

"All Too Well (Taylor's Version)" would be key to the mammoth
success of her re-recordings, sealing its position as an essential part
of her universe when it topped the *Billboard* Hot 100 on its release.

There were nine further "From the Vault" tracks—
some which had never previously been released,
others that had been given to other artists. Little Big
Town released "Better Man" in 2016, while "Babe"
was recorded by Sugarland in 2018.

> "I definitely feel more
> free to create now.
> And I'm making more
> albums at a more
> rapid pace than I ever
> did before, because
> I think the more art
> you create, hopefully
> the less pressure you
> put on yourself."

"Ronan" was initially a charity single for a 2012
Stand Up to Cancer telethon, in honor of a little boy,
Ronan Thompson, who died of neuroblastoma in
2011. Written from the heartaching point of view of
his mother, Maya, Taylor credited her as a co-writer,
having been inspired by her blog posts.

"Message in a Bottle" had originally been the
first song she wrote with Max Martin and Shellback
when working on *Red*, but it ended up on the cutting
room floor. Another previously unreleased track, "Nothing New,"
became an anxious ballad with Phoebe Bridgers, as they worry over
how the industry worships and then discards female musicians.

She teamed up again with Ed Sheeran on "Everything Has
Changed," and a new track, "Run," and dueted with Chris Stapleton
on "I Bet You Think About Me." Here she aimed snark at an ex for
his efforts in trying to remain hipster cool and relevant. She was also
self-aware in her acknowledgement that he would think her crazy for
writing a song about him. It was released as a single to country radio

stations, with an accompanying video directed by Blake Lively, in which she played up to her "Blank Space" persona as she hijacks the wedding of her ex.

Much of the promotion and merchandising focused on the ten-minute version of "All Too Well" and the autumnal aesthetics of the album. New artwork showed Taylor posing in a red vintage convertible, wearing a burgundy fisherman's cap and with her signature red lips. There was a red scarf available for sale on her website, and she partnered with Starbucks for a "Taylor's Latte" that customers could order.

As well as entering the *Billboard* 200 at No. 1 on its release on November 12, the album won Top Country Album at the *Billboard* Music Awards, while at the 2022 American Music Awards she was named

Artist of the Year, and at the 65th Annual Grammy Awards, *All Too Well: The Short Film* won for Best Music Video.

Taylor's tireless creative output continued when she announced the imminent arrival of her tenth album while picking up her award for Video of the Year at the MTV Video Music Awards for *All Too Well: The Short Film*. She followed up with a post explaining that this new album, *Midnights*, would be "the stories of 13 sleepless nights scattered throughout my life."

The idea of a sleepless night peppered her back catalog, with midnight being namechecked in "22," "Style," and "New Year's Day." The middle of the night was also a time for dreams and desires and terrors in tracks like ". . .Ready for It?" and "Better Man." There was the intimate happiness of "All Too Well," where they dance in the kitchen by the refrigerator light. In the final words of her album *Lover*, she expresses her wish to be defined by love, and not by things that keep her awake at night.

For Taylor it was a vulnerable, lonely time where late-night worries often drove her creative voice. Grappling with the devastation of bad love, the pressures she felt to be the good girl, the expectation placed

on her by society, and her often overwhelming desire for revenge on those who wronged her could take her to dark places. By choosing this theme for a concept album, with all the codes and references to previous music, it slotted into the retrospective feel of her re-recordings.

The roll-out of the album was a case study in perfect marketing, building up anticipation by dropping clues to its themes and content without releasing a beat of music. Through artwork reveals and a teaser of her upcoming videos, she hinted at not just a fairytale "magic at midnight" theme, but a seventies aesthetic of wood-paneled rooms, garish patterns, and plenty of mustard and maroon. Over seventeen days, as part of a "Midnights Mayhem" game on TikTok, she spun a vintage bingo cage, pulling out a random number and then revealing its corresponding track name on her retro dial phone.

Midnights was the first album she recorded entirely with Jack Antonoff, and while its content was dark, it was also a marker of a happier place, where she said, "I definitely feel more free to create now. And I'm making more albums at a more rapid pace than I ever did before, because I think the more art you create, hopefully the less pressure you put on yourself."

PAGE 134-135 Accepting the award for Best Long Form Video at the 2022 MTV Video Music Awards.

ABOVE Taylor Swift accepts the Favorite Pop Album award for *Red (Taylor's Version)* at the 2022 American Music Awards.

THE ESSENTIAL... TAYLOR SWIFT

Three hours after the album dropped at midnight on October 21, she put out a deluxe *3am Edition* of the album, which featured seven bonus tracks, creating a further frenzy—helping to break the Spotify record for the most streams of an album in a single day.

The album opened with the woozy "Lavender Haze." It was a return to the pop of *Lover* and *Reputation*, with synthesizers and beats rather than acoustic instruments, and with a haunting quality as she explored love and desire, regret and angst, and fantasies of revenge. If her other albums had been color-coded, then *Midnights* ran with it—from "Lavender Haze" to "Maroon" to the shimmering gold of "Bejeweled." "Maroon" used variations of the color to describe a long-distance romance, from the cheap rosé wine being drunk to the rust symbolic of the distance between phone lines, and the purple bruise of a love bite.

"Snow on the Beach" was a metaphor for strange, awe-inspiring love, with Lana Del Rey's vocals in the background. When she released a deluxe edition of the album, the track was re-recorded with more Lana Del Rey, following feedback that she could hardly be heard on the original.

There wasn't the big catchy hit of previous albums, although "Shake It Off" and "Me!" had felt a little out of step. But the lead single, "Anti-Hero," a track she described as one of her favorite songs she'd ever written, was a "guided tour" of what she hates about herself, as she comes to terms with her own fallibility. She is tormented with worries about her body and aging, that she might drive away another person in her life, and that she is the problem.

In the music video, set within her seventies world, she is led astray by her bad doppelgänger, has a strange fantasy in which her children are fighting over her will at her funeral, and bleeds out glitter. As she explained to director Martin McDonagh in an interview with *Variety*, "It's sort of a metaphor for how I don't feel like a normal person. I must have something wrong with me. And it's all the examples of disordered thinking."

Much of the appeal of the album was working out the sheer number of codes in song lyrics and music videos, as the references acted as "invisible strings" between moments in her past. "Bejeweled," for example, appeared to refer to her night at the Met Gala in 2016, when she tired of a thankless relationship and chose to shimmer and shine. The music video, which was a twist on Cinderella, featured

THE ESSENTIAL... TAYLOR SWIFT

OPPOSITE At the 2023 Grammy Awards where she scooped Best Music Video for *All Too Well: The Short Film*.

ABOVE Landing the double. *Midnights* and "Anti-Hero" both hit No. 1 in the Official Album and Official Singles charts respectively.

the band Haim as the ugly sisters, Laura Dern as the wicked stepmother, and, in Taylor's words, a "psychotic" amount of Easter eggs.

"High Infidelity," from the *3am Edition*, set social media abuzz with a reference to something significant happening on April 29. Was it at Gigi Hadid's party that she first met Joe Alwyn, or was it to do with Calvin Harris dropping "This Is What You Came For" that day—a song, it later transpired, she had written?

Throughout the album, she scrutinized her own ambition and what it took for her to get to where she is. "You're on Your Own, Kid" was a reflection of her journey from a small town to New York for her *1989* days, when she would try and fit in by hosting parties and starve herself to be thin. She juxtaposes the innocence of early fame with a cynicism that life isn't the fairy tale she thought it was. There's hope at the end, as she calls for her listeners to make friendship bracelets.

There were also two big revenge tracks, "Karma" and "Vigilante Shit," which took aim at those who had wronged her, including the feud with Scooter Braun and her previous record label. In the final, thirteenth track on the album, "Mastermind," she faces up to her manipulative, Machiavellian side and attributes it to her own insecurities. In the final twist, the boyfriend who she had plotted to be with smiles because he knew about her plans all along.

As part of her promotional tour, she appeared on *The Tonight Show Starring Jimmy Fallon*, where she offered up a hint that she might be touring soon. "I think I should do it," she said, to cheers from the audience. "When it's time," she added cryptically. Just a week later, on November 1, she made a special announcement that she would be going back on the road with The Eras Tour—an ambitious musical journey that would be the biggest of her career.

CHAPTER NINE

THE ERAS TOUR

At the beginning of November 2022, *Midnights* achieved an historic first—every spot in the Top Ten of the *Billboard* Hot 100 was filled by a track from the album. It was just one sign of how Taylor would dominate the music industry in 2023.

When tickets for the Eras Tour first went on sale, the unprecedented demand caused Ticketmaster to crash. But the record-breaking two million tickets sold on the first day were an early indication of just how overwhelming the global demand would be to see Taylor live.

Taylor trained for six months to prep for the tour, practicing her set list by singing while running on the treadmill every day. "I wanted to be so over rehearsed that I could be silly with the fans and not lose my train of thought," she said.

The tour was the largest undertaking of her career so far, with each three-and-a-half-hour show featuring forty-five songs, sixteen costume changes, six pyrotechnic displays, a long runway stage and elevated platform, and intricate set design to immerse the audience in her fantasy worlds that represented seventeen years' worth of music—the mossy cottagecore of *Folklore* and *Evermore*, the hazy purple of *Speak Now*, the gothic revenge of *Reputation*, and the sparkling, shimmering rainbows of *Lover*. She zipped from feverishly energetic to introspective acoustic, whether she was strapping a guitar around her neck or seated at the piano.

"They had to work really hard to get the tickets," she said of her fans. "I wanted to play a show that was longer than they ever thought it would be, because that makes me feel good leaving the stadium."

THE ESSENTIAL... TAYLOR SWIFT

"I wanted to be so over-rehearsed that I could be silly with the fans, and not lose my train of thought."

When the tour kicked off on March 17, 2023, in Glendale, Arizona, it had a more dramatic impact on the town's businesses than the 2023 Super Bowl, which was held at the same stadium. The tour gave a massive economic boost for whichever city she was playing in, with hotels and restaurants booked out from the demand of her vast audience.

"Beatlemania and *Thriller* have nothing on these shows," said Phoebe Bridgers, as it became the mass cultural moment of a generation. Fans wore and traded friendship bracelets, as she had encouraged in "You're on Your Own, Kid." They came dressed up as their favorite Taylor era, and it was calculated by *The Washington Post* that the average US fan would spend nearly $1,300 at each gig, which included tickets, food and drink, travel, and merchandise. Her show in Denver was said to have added $140 million to Colorado's GDP, and her influence on the Philadelphia economy was noted by the Federal Reserve. The "Taylor effect" also led to pleas from countries like Thailand for her to come and perform there.

Another ambitious element to her all-conquering year was bringing the Eras Tour to an even bigger audience by showing it in cinemas for all those who hadn't managed to get tickets. Rather than going with a traditional studio, she made a deal with the world's biggest cinema chain, AMC, to release *Taylor Swift: The Eras Tour*, and when the concert film arrived in cinemas on October 13, AMC recorded its highest ever single-day ticket sales.

The Eras Tour was one element of what she referred to as "a three-part summer of feminine extravaganza," alongside the box-office phenomenon of Greta Gerwig's *Barbie* and Beyoncé's

Renaissance World Tour, which followed a similar AMC deal when it came to cinemas.

During her shows in Nashville in May, her screaming audience received the breaking news that *Speak Now (Taylor's Version)* would be arriving on July 7. The new album cover, with Taylor in a purple dress similar to the one from the original 2010 album, was flashed onto the big screen as she launched into "Sparks Fly" as the surprise song of the night. Shortly after, she posted on her social media accounts that it was arriving "just in time for July 9th, iykyk [if you know you know]." It was a little nod to fans about the date mentioned in the lyrics of "Last Kiss."

As with the other re-recordings, she stayed true to the original, except for one controversial line in "Better than Revenge," where she tweaked the slut-shaming to a less judgmental narrative. The "From the Vault" tracks were once again produced by Aaron Dessner and Jack Antonoff, and she collaborated with era-defining emo-rock musicians Fall Out Boy on "Electric Touch" and Paramore's Hayley Williams on "Castles Crumbling" to add further late 2000s nostalgia.

ABOVE Channeling the "Lavender Haze" of her *Midnights* era.

OPPOSITE A nod to *Reputation* with an outfit styled with snake motifs.

"When Emma Falls in Love" was a sweet piano ballad that some thought was an ode to her friend the actress Emma Stone, and "I Can See You," which boasted an infectious electric guitar, sounded like a mix between the tracks "Mine" and "You Belong with Me." She premiered the music video during her gig in Kansas City, and the spy-themed narrative featured her ex Taylor Lautner, who had come off well in the song that was said to have been written about him "Back to December." However, when she performed "Dear John" as part of her Minneapolis show in June, she urged her fans to show kindness to her famous targets who hadn't fared quite as well.

Speak Now (Taylor's Version) debuted at No. 1 on the *Billboard* 200, making her the woman with the most chart-topping albums in history.

On August 9, in Inglewood, California, the last US date on her tour (before moving on to Mexico and South America), and wearing a long blue dress that referenced the colors of its new artwork, she announced that *1989 (Taylor's Version)* would be coming soon. It was released on October 27, 2023, nine years after the original turned her into a pop phenomenon. Taylor's version now included five new synthy "From the Vault" tracks, which added extra insight to the romantic longing she felt during this period.

"Is It Over Now?" was about a relationship fracturing from resentment and betrayal, and a hit at Harry Styles with the mention of a blue dress on a boat, blood on snow alluding to a snowmobile accident from "Out of the Woods," and his searching for a replacement in every model's bed. "Say Don't Go" was about the pain of being led on by someone who had no intention of committing, and which leaves her bleeding from their twisting knife.

"'Slut!'" was a message to her critics that she was too wrapped up in love to care about what they think. With the flamingo pink sunrise and the aquamarine of the pool, and her lovestruck infatuation with the boy who everyone wants, it also had *Lover* vibes.

With its entry at the top of the *Billboard* 200, this release was Taylor's thirteenth No. 1 album, and she broke her own record for the most streams on a single day on Spotify by an artist. And by achieving her biggest ever sales week for an album, with 3.5 million units sold around the world, it was an even greater success than the original.

"This is the proudest and happiest I've ever felt, and the most creatively fulfilled and free I've ever been."

"This is the proudest and happiest I've ever felt, and the most creatively fulfilled and free I've ever been," she said in late 2023. She had dominated the year, becoming a billion-dollar phenomenon and saturating every aspect of pop culture.

At the time of the release of *Midnights*, the status of her relationship with Joe Alwyn was still shrouded in mystery. No one knew whether or not they were engaged, but what was gathered from the album was that they were still blissfully together. There were a couple of tracks that appeared to offer this reassurance, "Lavender Haze" and "Sweet Nothing," a song which he co-wrote as William Bowery, and appeared to reveal the protective space of their domestic set-up.

Taylor was also dismayed that her marital status was constantly up for discussion. In "Midnight Rain" she thinks of the partners who didn't get how much her dreams meant to her, with lyrics that take aim at outdated stereotypes about ambition being a male-only pursuit.

There was a huge surprise when a source revealed in April 2023 that they had, in fact, split. It was quickly followed by speculation that she was now dating Matty Healy of The 1975, when he was spotted at some of the shows. The rumors left many Swifties angry and upset, given his propensity for making controversial statements, including those aimed at the rapper Ice Spice. She later joined Taylor on stage at one of her shows, and they then teamed up on a remix of "Karma," which some believed was Taylor's "damage control" of the situation.

When Taylor went public with her romance with Travis Kelce, the Kansas City Chiefs NFL star, in October, it brought to life the

themes of "Stay Stay Stay"—the love between the good girl and an American football player.

In televised matches, Taylor was shown enthusiastically cheering him on in a private box, either next to his mother or with her famous friends. Her appearances at his games brought a massive increase in viewership for the NFL and a cross-pollination of pop and sport.

In an interview in *Time* in December 2023, as she was named the magazine's Person of the Year, she revealed that they had started dating when she found out he had turned up to one of her shows wearing a friendship bracelet with his telephone number in it.

If her six-year relationship with Joe had been defined by its privacy, she would embrace being fully in the spotlight with Travis—supporting him at his games, embracing him on the pitch, making a surprise appearance on the same episode of *Saturday Night Live*, holding hands when going out to dinner, and during one of her shows in Argentina, she changed lyrics to "Karma is the guy on the Chiefs."

ABOVE LEFT Taking to the stage with Ice Spice at MetLife Stadium on May 27, 2023 in East Rutherford, New Jersey.

ABOVE RIGHT New love interest American football star Travis Kelce.

ABOVE Taylor Swift accepts the Album of the Year award for *Midnights* at the 2024 Grammys, where she also announces her eleventh studio album, *The Tortured Poets Department*, to be released on April 19, 2024.

"When you say a relationship is public, that means I'm going to see him do what he loves, we're showing up for each other, other people are there and we don't care," she said.

The Eras Tour continued into 2024, with shows across Asia and Europe, further building on the mythology of the "Swiftiverse." She won the Grammy for Album of the Year for *Midnights*—making her the first artist ever to win it four times. And on top of this she announced a new album, *The Tortured Poets Department*, that same night.

Across her genre-shifting career, she revealed her own story through music, using her experiences to shape her own narrative worlds. Her song lyrics could be pieced together like an Agatha Christie novel, leading to a fixation by her fan base on every minuscule detail or clue she dropped. As a businesswoman, she built an empire worth over $1 billion, and she continues to dominate news headlines and social media as she deftly utilizes every modern marketing tool at her disposal. Now that she has reclaimed her own music and boosted global economies, she continues to be a guiding light for female musicians—and to demonstrate the power of storytelling.

Taylor Swift (2006)

Track List
1. Tim McGraw
2. Picture to Burn
3. Teardrops on My Guitar
4. A Place in This World
5. Cold as You
6. The Outside
7. Tied Together with a Smile
8. Stay Beautiful
9. Should've Said No
10. Mary's Song (Oh My My My)
11. Our Song

Recorded
Castles; Quad; Sound Cottage;
Sound Emporium (Nashville)

Released
October 24, 2006

Label
Big Machine

Notes
"If Taylor Swift retired right after dropping her debut album, she'd still be remembered as a legend today [...] Taylor debuted with complete mastery of a genre she was also completely transforming." *Rolling Stone*

The commercial success of Taylor Swift's debut album was partly attributed to her online marketing strategy. While a familiar tactic to pop and hip hop artists, Taylor Swift was the first country artist to promote her songs on social media platforms, and it brought her a loyal fan base.

Fearless (2008)

Track List

1. Fearless
2. Fifteen
3. Love Story
4. Hey Stephen
5. White Horse
6. You Belong with Me
7. Breathe (featuring Colbie Caillat)
8. Tell Me Why
9. You're Not Sorry
10. The Way I Loved You
11. Forever & Always
12. The Best Day
13. Change

Recorded
Blackbird; Fool on the Hill; Quad; Sound Cottage; Sound Emporium; Starstruck (Nashville); Sound Kitchen (Franklin)

Released
November 11, 2008

Label
Big Machine

Notes

Swift began re-recording her first six studio albums in November 2020. The decision came after a public dispute between her and the music executive Scooter Braun, who acquired the masters of Swift's first six studio albums —which Swift had been trying to buy for years—following her departure from Big Machine Records in November 2018.

Fearless (Taylor's Version) is the first re-recorded album, released on April 9, 2021 by Republic. It includes re-recordings of the tracks on *Fearless* (2008), the soundtrack single "Today Was a Fairytale" from the 2010 film *Valentine's Day*, and six previously unreleased "From the Vault" tracks: "You All Over Me" (featuring Maren Morris); "Mr. Perfectly Fine"; "We Were Happy"; "That's When" (featuring Keith Urban); "Don't You"; and "Bye Bye Baby."

OPPOSITE
Celebrating at the 2010 Grammy Awards with her mom (R).

Speak Now (2010)

Track List

1. Mine
2. Sparks Fly
3. Back to December
4. Speak Now
5. Dear John
6. Mean
7. The Story of Us
8. Never Grow Up
9. Enchanted
10. Better than Revenge
11. Innocent
12. Haunted
13. Last Kiss
14. Long Live

Recorded

Aimeeland; Blackbird; Pain in the Art; Starstruck (Nashville); Capitol (Hollywood); Stonehurst (Bowling Green)

Released

October 25, 2010

Label

Big Machine

OPPOSITE
Opening night of the Speak Now Tour in the UK, 2011.

Notes

On May 5, 2023, at the first Eras Tour show in Nashville, Swift announced *Speak Now (Taylor's Version)* and its release date of July 7, 2023. It is the third re-recorded album. The six previously unreleased "From the Vault" tracks include: "Electric Touch" (featuring Fall Out Boy); "When Emma Falls in Love"; "I Can See You"; "Castles Crumbling" (featuring Hayley Williams); "Foolish One"; and "Timeless."

Red (2012)

Track List

1. State of Grace
2. Red
3. Treacherous
4. I Knew You Were Trouble
5. All Too Well
6. 22
7. I Almost Do
8. We Are Never Ever Getting Back Together
9. Stay Stay Stay
10. The Last Time (featuring Gary Lightbody of Snow Patrol)
11. Holy Ground
12. Sad Beautiful Tragic
13. The Lucky One
14. Everything Has Changed (featuring Ed Sheeran)
15. Starlight
16. Begin Again

OPPOSITE
At the 2013 American Music Awards.

Recorded

Blackbird; Pain in the Art (Nashville); Ballroom West (New York); Instrument Landing (Minneapolis); MXM (Stockholm); Conway, Village (Los Angeles); Garage (Topanga Canyon); Ruby Red (Atlanta

Released
October 22, 2012

Label
Big Machine

Notes
On June 18, 2021, Swift announced *Red (Taylor's Version)*. Released by Republic on November 12, 2021, it includes nine "From the Vault" tracks: "Better Man"; "Nothing New" (featuring Phoebe Bridgers); "Babe"; "Message in a Bottle"; "I Bet You Think About Me" (featuring Chris Stapleton); "Forever Winter"; "Run" (featuring Ed Sheeran); "The Very First Night"; and "All Too Well (10 Minute Version)."

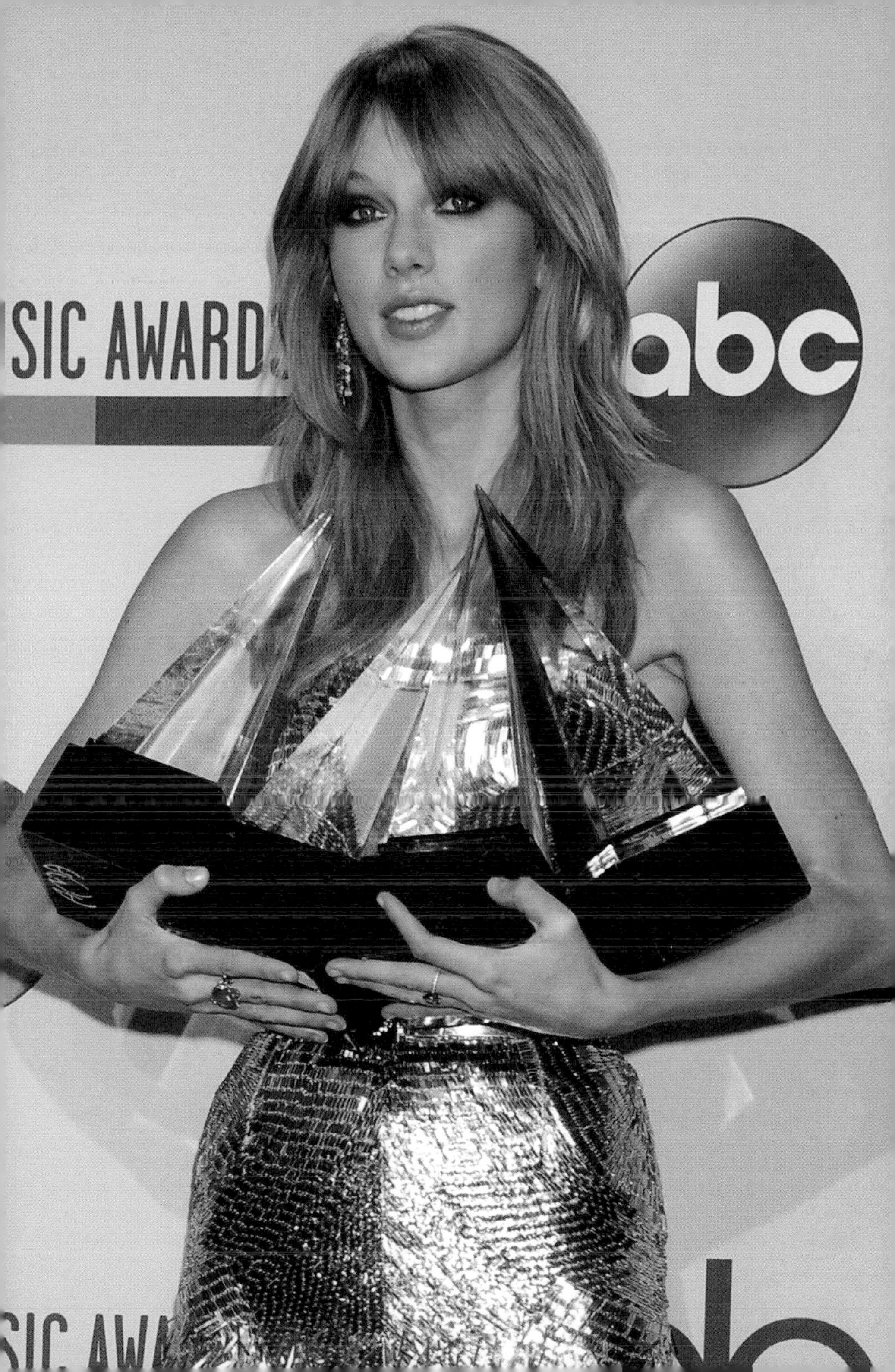
abc

1989 (2014)

Track List

1. Welcome to New York
2. Blank Space
3. Style
4. Out of the Woods
5. All You Had to Do Was Stay
6. Shake It Off
7. I Wish You Would
8. Bad Blood
9. Wildest Dreams
10. How You Get the Girl
11. This Love
12. I Know Places
13. Clean

Recorded

Conway Recording (Los Angeles); Jungle City (New York City); Lamby's House (Brooklyn); MXM (Stockholm); Pain in the Art (Nashville); Elevator Nobody (Göteborg); The Hideaway (London)

Released

October 27, 2014

Label

Big Machine

Notes

Swift released the re-recording of *1989 (Taylor's Version)* on October 27, 2023, nine years after the original release of *1989*. There are five previously unreleased "From the Vault" tracks: "'Slut!'"; "Say Don't Go"; "Now That We Don't Talk"; "Suburban Legends"; and "Is It Over Now?" The record was Spotify's most-streamed album in a single day for 2023, and of all time on Amazon Music. In the US, *1989 (Taylor's Version)* was Swift's thirteenth No. 1 album on the *Billboard* 200.

OPPOSITE
Taylor Swift during her epic 1989 Times Square concert in 2014.

Reputation (2017)

Track List
1. ...Ready For It?
2. End Game (featuring Ed Sheeran and Future)
3. I Did Something Bad
4. Don't Blame Me
5. Delicate
6. Look What You Made Me Do
7. So It Goes...
8. Gorgeous
9. Getaway Car
10. King of My Heart
11. Dancing with Our Hands Tied
12. Dress
13. This Is Why We Can't Have Nice Things
14. Call It What You Want
15. New Year's Day

Recorded
Conway Recording (Los Angeles); MXM (Los Angeles/Stockholm); Rough Customer (Brooklyn); Seismic Activities (Portland); Tree Sound (Atlanta)

Released
November 10, 2017

Label
Big Machine

Notes
Reputation was Taylor Swift's last album under Big Machine Records and was considered her "comeback" album in response to the fallout from the West–Kardashian controversy and the infamously leaked phone call. Darker and edgier than anything previously released, the album is Taylor Swift's least commercially successful. Its lead single, "Look What You Made Me Do," was released on August 24, 2017, peaking at No. 1 on the *Billboard* Hot 100. The accompanying music video broke the record for the most 24-hour views on YouTube. It was Taylor Swift's first No. 1 on the UK Singles Chart.

Lover (2019)

Track List

1. I Forgot That You Existed
2. Cruel Summer
3. Lover
4. The Man
5. The Archer
6. I Think He Knows
7. Miss Americana & the Heartbreak Prince
8. Paper Rings
9. Cornelia Street
10. Death by a Thousand Cuts
11. London Boy
12. Soon You'll Get Better (featuring The Dixie Chicks)
13. False God
14. You Need to Calm Down
15. Afterglow
16. Me! (featuring Brendon Urie of Panic! at the Disco)
17. It's Nice to Have a Friend
18. Daylight

Recorded

Conway Recording (Los Angeles); Electric Lady (New York City); Golden Age West (Auckland); Golden Age (Los Angeles); Electric Feel (Los Angeles); Metropolis (London)

Released

August 23, 2019

Label

Republic

OPPOSITE
At the 2019 MTV Video Music Awards.

Notes

Lover is an album filled with love and hope. It marks a return to her familiar style of songwriting exploring love and emotional intimacy, and along with the album cover's aesthetics of pastel colors, rejects the gritty harder edge of its predecessor.

"*Lover*, her reassuringly strong seventh album, is a palate cleanse, a recalibration and a reaffirmation of old strengths. It's a transitional album designed to close one particularly bruised chapter and suggest ways to move forward—or in some cases, to return to how things once were." Jon Caramanica *New York Times*

Folklore (2020)

Track List
1. The 1
2. Cardigan
3. The Last Great American Dynasty
4. Exile (featuring Bon Iver)
5. My Tears Ricochet
6. Mirrorball
7. Seven
8. August
9. This Is Me Trying
10. Illicit Affairs
11. Invisible String
12. Mad Woman
13. Epiphany
14. Betty
15. Peace
16. Hoax

Recorded
Conway (Los Angeles); Kitty Committee (Los Angeles); Electric Lady (New York City); Long Pond (Hudson Valley); Rough Customer (Brooklyn)

Released
July 24, 2020

Label
Republic

Notes
A surprise album, released on July 24, 2020, following the COVID-19 pandemic in early 2020, *Folklore* was conceived and written during quarantine, working with producers Aaron Dessner and Jack Antonoff virtually, and recording vocals in a home studio in Los Angeles. It won Album of the Year at the 63rd Annual Grammy Awards in 2021, making Taylor Swift the first woman in history to win the honor three times, having previously scooped the award in 2009 for *Fearless* and 2015 for *1989*.

OPPOSITE
At the 2021 Grammy Awards.

Evermore (2020)

Track List
1. Willow
2. Champagne Problems
3. Gold Rush
4. 'Tis the Damn Season
5. Tolerate It
6. No Body, No Crime (featuring Haim)
7. Happiness
8. Dorothea
9. Coney Island (featuring the National)
10. Ivy
11. Cowboy like Me
12. Long Story Short
13. Marjorie
14. Closure
15. Evermore (featuring Bon Iver)

Recorded
Kitty Committee (Los Angeles); Long Pond (Hudson Valley); Scarlet Pimpernel (Exeter); Ariel Rechtshaid's house (Los Angeles)

Released
December 11, 2020

Label
Republic

Notes
Another surprise album, *Evermore* was released less than five months after *Folklore* and is considered to be its sister album. Taylor Swift announced the album via social media shortly before her thirty-first birthday, writing: "You've all been so caring, supportive and thoughtful on my birthdays and so this time I thought I would give you something! I also know this holiday season will be a lonely one for most of us and if there are any of you out there who turn to music to cope with missing loved ones the way I do, this is for you."

OPPOSITE
Scoring her second No. 1 of 2020 on the UK's Official Albums Chart with *Evermore*.

Midnights (2022)

Track List
1. Lavender Haze
2. Maroon
3. Anti-Hero
4. Snow on the Beach (featuring Lana Del Rey)
5. You're on Your Own, Kid
6. Midnight Rain
7. Question...?
8. Vigilante Shit
9. Bejeweled
10. Labyrinth
11. Karma
12. Sweet Nothing
13. Mastermind

Recorded
Electric Lady (New York City); Henson Recording (Los Angeles); Rough Customer (Brooklyn)

Released
October 21, 2022

Label
Republic

Notes
"It's an album that's cool, collected and mature. It's also packed with fantastic songs and at a slight remove from everything else currently happening in pop's upper echelons. As ever, you wouldn't like to predict what Taylor Swift will do next, but what she's doing at the moment is very good indeed." Alexis Petridis *The Guardian*

Inspired by her sleepless nights, *Midnights* is Taylor Swift's tenth studio album. Her eleventh consecutive No. 1 album on the *Billboard* 200 and her fifth to sell over one million first-week copies, it was also 2022's best-selling album.

OPPOSITE
Winning Album of the Year at the 2023 MTV Video Music Awards.

The Tortured Poets Department (2024)

Track List

1. Fortnight (featuring Post Malone)
2. The Tortured Poets Department
3. My Boy Only Breaks His Favorite Toys
4. Down Bad
5. So Long, London
6. But Daddy I Love Him
7. Fresh Out the Slammer
8. Florida!!! (featuring Florence + the Machine)
9. Guilty as Sin?
10. Who's Afraid of Little Old Me?
11. I Can Fix Him (No Really I Can)
12. loml
13. I Can Do It with a Broken Heart
14. The Smallest Man Who Ever Lived
15. The Alchemy
16. Clara Bow
17. Bonus track: The Manuscript

Recorded
2022-2023

Released
April 19, 2024

Label
Republic

Notes

The Tortured Poets Department is the eleventh studio album from Taylor Swift. After winning Best Pop Vocal Album for *Midnights* at the 2024 Grammys, she dropped the bombshell announcement of the forthcoming release during her acceptance speech. Earlier, Taylor Swift had updated her profile picture across her social media platforms—a tactic she has used before to signal a new album—but many fans were anticipating the announcement of *Reputation (Taylor's Version)* so much so that the hashtag #RepTV was trending ahead of the televised ceremony. The next day she posted the album's track listing to her social media accounts, prompting fans to start their detective work deciphering each song's meaning.

SOURCES

Billboard, The Buffalo News, Business Insider, Elle, Entertainment Weekly, Esquire, Forbes, GQ, The Guardian, Los Angeles Times, Marie Claire, The New Yorker, The New York Times, NME, People, The Philadelphia Inquirer, Philadelphia Magazine, Pitchfork, Rolling Stone, Slant, Time, USA Today, Vanity Fair, Variety, Vogue, Vox, Vulture.

PICTURE CREDITS

T: Top; B: Bottom; L: Left; R: Right

ALAMY: Cover Xavier Collin/Image Press Agency **P6** AP Photo/Mark Humphrey **P11, P57** John Barrett/PHOTOlink **P16** © Renee Jones Schneider/Minneapolis Star Tribune/ZUMAPRESS.com **P18** ARCHIVIO GBB **P20, P69T** ZUMA Press, Inc. **P39, P48, P54B** Associated Press **P44, P52** Rodolfo Sassano **P50** Sayre Berman **P51** Moviestore Collection Ltd **P54TL, P90** WENN Rights Ltd **P54TR, P60** PA Images, **P62** Aflo Co. Ltd, **P64-65** Charles Sykes/Invision/AP, **P69B** Storms Media Group **P71** Barry Brecheisen/Invision/AP **P81** Grzegorz Czapski **P113** © Netflix / courtesy Everett Collection **P114** Abaca Press **P115** Courtesy of MTV via Sipa USA **P116** © Disney+ / Courtesy Everett Collection **P119, P148T** AP Photo/Chris Pizzello **P169, P174** Jordan Strauss/Invision/AP **P173** John Angelillo/UPI **GETTY: P4** Jeff Kravitz/TAS23/Getty Images for TAS Rights Management **P9T, P36T, P46, P128, P157, P162, P165** Kevin Mazur/WireImage **P9BL** John Shearer/WireImage **P9BR** Jeffrey Ufberg/WireImage **P10** TAS2023 **P12, P88, P103** John Shearer/AMA2019 **P14-15, P17, P142** Buda Mendes/TAS23 **P22** © 2014 NBAE, photo by Jesse D. Garrabrant/NBAE **P23** Gardiner Anderson/Bauer-Griffin/GC Images **P24L, P34** Rick Diamond/WireImage for CMT **P24R** Christopher Polk/ACMA2010 **P27** Michael Caulfield/WireImage **P28, P30** Michael Buckner **P32** Ethan Miller **P35** Kevin Winter/ACMA **P36BR** Larry Busacca/Getty Images for NARAS **P40** Jason Kempin **P42** Dimitrios Kambouris/WireImage for Clear Channel Radio New York **P43** Jason Kempin/Getty Images for Erickson Public Relations **P53TL, P53B, P78L** Larry Busacca **P57** Mark Metcalfe/TAS **P58** James Devaney/GC Images **P66, P67, P78R** Alo Ceballos/GC Images **P70** Samir Hussein **P73T** Larry Busacca/MTV1415 **P73BL** Dan MacMedan/WireImage **P73BR** Kevin Mazur/BMA2015/WireImage **P74, P86** Gareth Cattermole/TAS18 **P79** Jackson Lee/GC Images **P80** Joe Mahoney **P82, P140, P151** Kevin Winter/Getty Images for TAS **P84, P138, P145, P152L** Kevin Mazur/TAS **P85T** Don Arnold/TAS18 **P85B, P144, P146-147, P148B** John Shearer/TAS **P92, P97, P131** Kevin Mazur/Getty Images for iHeartMedia **P93** Jeff Kravitz/2019 iHeartMedia **P95, P102R** Kevin Winter/Getty Images for dcp **P98-99** Rich Fury/Getty Images for iHeartMedia **P100** Kevin Mazur/Getty Images for Ithaca Holdings **P101** Kevin Mazur/Getty Images for ABA **P102L, P104, P105** Kevin Mazur/AMA2019 **P106** Daniele Venturelli/WireImage **P108** Theo Wargo/WireImage **P118L&R** TAS Rights Management 2021 **P120-121** Jay L. Clendenin / Los Angeles Times **P122** Kevin Mazur/Getty Images for The Recording Academy **P124, P134-135** Jeff Kravitz/Getty Images for MTV/Paramount Global **P126** Kevin Mazur/Getty Images for The Rock and Roll Hall of Fame **P127** Evan Agostini/Invision/AP **P130B, P132** Matt Winkelmeyer/TAS18 **P136** John Shearer/Getty Images for The Recording Academy **P152R** Gotham/GC Images **P153** Johnny Nunez/Getty Images for The Recording Academy **P154** Al Messerschmidt **P158** Dave Hogan **P161** Gregg DeGuire/WireImage **P166** Jamie McCarthy/Getty Images for MTV **SHUTTERSTOCK: P29, P53TR** Startraks **P36BL** Kpa/Zuma **P76** Broadimage **P110** Chelsea Lauren **P112** Alberto Reyes **P137, P170** OfficialCharts.com